MARY MACK

# MARY MACKILLOP

## The Ground of Her Loving

**Margaret Paton**

DARTON · LONGMAN + TODD

First published in 2010 by
Darton, Longman and Todd Ltd
1 Spencer Court
140 – 142 Wandsworth High Street
London SW18 4JJ

ISBN: 978-0-232-52799-5

A catalogue record for this book is available from the British Library

Phototypeset by Kerrypress Ltd, Luton, Bedfordshire
Printed and bound in Great Britain by CPI Antony Rowe, Chippenham

# Contents

# Introduction

Many books have been written about Mary MacKillop (1842–1909), an Australian of Scottish descent. They are mostly books about her remarkable life. One can read and re-read the story of her life, and in the year of her Canonisation there will be more interest in her life than ever, particularly by those in countries other than Australia, although there are Australians too who know little about her life.

The title, *The Ground of Her Loving*, was inspired by Paul Tillich's phrase, *the ground of being*, by which he meant the reason or reasons for being. Such an abstract phrase would hardly be appropriate as a title for a book about Mary MacKillop, who is earthy and practical. She is more concerned with loving than being. Her reasons for loving are the Sacred Heart of Jesus that was pierced for love, and the will of a God of great goodness who loves the poor, especially poor children.

*The Spirituality of Mary MacKillop* is the sub-title. Spirituality is not an easy word. By spirituality I mean the relation between the whole person, body, mind and spirit, and God. God comes into every part of a person's life. Daniel Lyne has written a book on Mary MacKillop's spirituality and I am indebted to him. I have tried to draw out the salient points of her spirituality in connection with the Will of God, humility, poverty, the Sacred Heart, obedience, unity, Eucharist and friendship and courage.

As I studied Mary MacKillop's spirituality, I have discovered that she had ideas in common with other spiritual writers. For example, the French philosopher, Simone Weil, regarding our attentive response to the Will of God and the concept of affliction. Evelyn Underhill, who wrote, as Mary MacKillop did, about the adorable Will of God. And Helen Prejean, who is still alive, and with whom Mary MacKillop courageously shared a willingness to be with those who were in prison, facing the death penalty, that few, if any, writers, have acknowledged adequately.

The contents of this book have been accumulating since 1997. It seems a very slight book to have taken so long to come together but I wrote as and when I was inspired and could find time. It is in the form of a series of articles that I trust will give the reader a sense of her articulate intelligence, which enabled her to stand her ground against bishops, the loving advice she gave to the Sisters, and her generosity of spirit which led her to forgive everyone who had wronged her.

The book has a theme, namely: what contemporary relevance has Mary MacKillop? It breaks down into a series of questions: What can she teach us about spirituality? What can we learn from her about Religious life and about her experience of life? It is really a book of much needed revisiting of concepts that have tended to lose their significance in this post-modern age, such as obedience, humility, and the Will of God. It is also a book whose theological approach is experiential rather than theoretical.

An ego-less life is one in which there is a total absence of self-importance, and no desire for her own way to prevail. Mary MacKillop's life was ego-less because she was open and welcoming to whatever was to be. The spirituality of an ego-less life reveals the nearness of God to her and the distance of the self. She had completely given herself into the hands of God – so completely that she feared she might do something that would be contrary to the Will of God. The aim of Chapter 1 is to show the extent of the opposition she had to endure from many bishops and priests.

Two articles on the Will of God are included. 'Mary MacKillop and the Will of God' (Chapter 2) was published in the *Australian Catholic Record* in December 1997. 'Living Creatively with the Will of God – Mary MacKillop and Evelyn Underhill' (Chapter 3) has not been published before. Mary herself was so committed to the Will of God. It was the centre of her life. I argue in 'Mary MacKillop and the Will of God' that it is her undivided devotion to the Will of God that is the key to understanding her holiness and why she is to be Canonised as Australia's first saint. The first paper is theoretical; the second is more experiential. The common, creative approach of Mary MacKillop and Evelyn Underhill to the

Will of God is remarkably similar, even to the use of the word 'adorable' in relation to the Will of God. I introduce the phrase, 'living with the Will of God' to highlight the question: What was it like for Mary MacKillop and Evelyn Underhill to experience and live with the Will of God? It was a creative challenge to both in spite of the negative language that was associated with the Will of God, such as 'submitting' and 'acquiescing'. I maintain that there are some expressive words that have a more positive and creative sense of being open to the Will of God than some of the negative words that have been used and may still have a lingering impact on our understanding of the Will of God. For Mary MacKillop, who used such words as 'dear', 'adorable' and 'beautiful' of the Will of God, this creative language would have been acceptable.

Chapter 4, 'Revisiting the Virtue of Humility with Mary MacKillop', was published in 2005. It has often been said that Mary was not concerned with theoretical matters because she was so practical. However, she was certainly interested in the concept of humility. She made a relevant distinction between true and false humility. False humility is a self-centred preoccupation with presenting oneself to others as a very humble person. True humility, on the other hand, is inspired by charity and thoughtfulness for others and putting oneself last. This is a very helpful distinction for us today as we still wrestle with the meaning of humility. Mary MacKillop frequently spoke of humility in connection with obedience and unity, both of which she believed her Sisters needed to take to the Sacred Heart in prayer. There is much that we can learn from Mary MacKillop about humility.

Daniel Lyne says that Mary MacKillop accepted poverty, whether material or spiritual, with a sense of joy. However, it would be a mistake to think that she rejoiced in poverty for its own sake. It was always in relation to the Will of God or the poverty of Christ that she wanted poverty for the Institute. Poverty was the hallmark of the Institute. However, it would have been very difficult to talk about Mary MacKillop's views on poverty without also taking into account Julian Tenison Woods' views. To begin with they were very much of the same mind about poverty and never owning property. But I felt, in Chapter 5, that there was a need to clarify the meaning of 'poverty' and 'poor' as they were using the terms. Mary MacKillop spoke frequently about poverty and being poor. It was spiritual poverty that was the centre of her interest. Sisters living in community were very often 'strapped for cash' and did not know where their next meal was coming from. They had to trust in God and recognise their dependence upon God. Today all the Sisters have enough to eat and they have a monthly budget. So, when they take a vow of poverty, what exactly are they vowing? One thing they are certainly vowing is to be detached from material possessions. Only if they are detached will they be able to follow the poor Christ, as Mary MacKillop wanted them to. In the time of the early Sisters, poverty was more of a reality for them than it is for us today. Mary MacKillop herself spoke of how hard it was to get money.

Chapter 6, 'Mary MacKillop's Heart and the Sacred Heart', is intended as a tribute to her love of the Heart of Christ. Worship of the Sacred Heart is no longer as prominent today as it was in the time of Mary MacKillop. 'Heart' is no longer considered to be an important word. However, Karl Rahner calls it a 'primordial' word. I call the word 'sacred' a connecting word. It connects precious experiences, that we wish to honour, with the Sacred Heart. I argue, following Karl Rahner, that a spirituality of the Heart of Jesus is urgently needed in the loveless world of today. Mary MacKillop's own heart of love can lead us in the direction of recovering a role for the Sacred Heart today, particularly in the Eucharist.

Mary MacKillop thought very highly of Ignatius Loyola, especially his letter on obedience. Obedience is a much misunderstood term today. Obedience was important to Mary MacKillop because she followed Ignatius in maintaining that obedience was essential for unity. She was keenly aware that her own Institute lacked the unity she wanted and she may have been afraid that it would grow progressively more disunited. She wanted all her Sisters to know that the source of their unity was their oneness in God and she wanted them to realise just how superficial their differences of opinion really were. I argue in Chapter 7 that obedience is a much needed virtue in Religious life today, as well as in everyday life, but it is important that we know what obedience really means.

Friendship seemed a good topic to include. When Mary became a religious and took her vows, she certainly did not give up her humanity. I know that there are different views about the place of friendship in the life of a religious. My own view is that friendship is a gift from God. Mary's friendship with Joanna Barr Smith, a Protestant, the subject of Chapter 8, was a deepening of her human experience. She became her friend when she recognised Joanna's spiritual difficulties and hoped that she would convert to the Catholic faith. Joanna remained a Protestant but she was a very generous and devoted friend to Mary. There was a bond of affection between them, which helped Mary to be a more understanding person, without in any way diminishing her holiness.

'Wisdom' is not a word that is very often used of Mary MacKillop. In Chapter 9, I have found plenty of evidence to show that she did indeed have wisdom. I discovered two core meanings to wisdom. The first is friendship with God – that is how the writer of the Wisdom of Solomon defines wisdom. The second is ordinariness and practical common sense. I argue that Mary MacKillop had wisdom in both these senses. It is her friendship with God that inspires her love of ordinariness. There can be no pretence, or affectation, with God. She knew that she was just herself with God.

Wisdom in the second sense is much more concerned with living life. Mary's wisdom in this sense resided in her gifts of gratitude, reconciliation and a sense of justice. Her lovely saying, 'Gratitude is the memory of the heart', enshrines so much wisdom. Her ability to forgive even her enemies has led Bishop Cuskelly to say that she is a saint of reconciliation for the world. Justice, for Mary, has to do with equality and dignity. But her wisdom in relation to punishment shows her compassionate nature and her realisation of *need*, not punishment, as a central part of the human condition that was the focus of her attention. Being attentive to the needs of others is a Gospel value full of wisdom and compassion.

Mary MacKillop was firstly an educationalist but throughout her Religious life she was involved in social work. She was concerned mainly with setting up Providences and Refuges for women who had fallen on evil days. Helen Prejean is a nun from the community of St Joseph in Medaille, Louisiana, with whom Mary MacKillop had one thing in common: courage, the subject of Chapter 10. I was impressed when I heard Helen Prejean speaking in Sydney against the death penalty in 2004. She had accompanied six men to the death chamber. Two of them were later found to be innocent. I was amazed to find, when I looked into Mary MacKillop's social work at the beginning of the Institute in Adelaide, that she had done prison visiting that had included visiting some inmates who were condemned to death. So great was her effect on a man called Fagan that he repented of his crime. Mary asked if she could go to the place of execution with him but it was not allowed. Unlike Helen Prejean, who went to the death chamber with the prisoners, Mary MacKillop could only ask to go with Fagan; but the fact that she was prepared to go so far with him is an example of her courage, which was all the more remarkable given that she was a woman and it was the late 1860s, when men liked women to know their place.

These are spiritual topics, for they are all concerned with Mary MacKillop, the whole person, and her relationship with God. I have endeavoured to bring them all together as the ground or reason of her loving, as the title of this book suggests.

# 1

## *A Selfless Life*

'*Mary MacKillop, profoundly God-centred, aware of the spiritual presence of that God from her childhood, allowed her awareness to spill over into loving service of others.*'

Colleen O'Sullivan RSJ

Mary MacKillop was an Australian who co-founded the Sisters of St Joseph of the Sacred Heart in 1866. The Order grew because it was needed. There were 750 Sisters in the Order[1] when she died at Mount Street, Sydney, on 8 August 1909. Even in her dying she was deemed to be a saint. Cardinal Moran,[2] who came to see her a few days before she died, left saying that he had attended the deathbed of a saint. The Cardinal presided at her funeral Mass. In his homily he spoke words that are just as true for today:

> It was a glorious apostolate Mother Mary has assigned to them (the Sisters) and it pleased God that the lowly seed sown in humility and poverty in those days of the ostentation of wealth and the pursuit of pleasure should grow into the stately tree it is today ...[3]

Today there are over a thousand Associates, as well as Sisters, who live the charism of Mary MacKillop, to do the Will of God with love and gratitude, in their day to day lives.

Who is this remarkable woman who has inspired so many to pray through her intercession for their needs?

She lived an 'ego-less' life that attracted opposition, as a mountain accumulates clouds. She always wanted what God wanted and saw each person as being on a pathway chosen for them by God. She spoke about the 'thorny yet strangely sweet path marked out for each of us to follow'.[4] It is the juxtaposition of her compassion with the patriarchal insensitivity of the Australian Church in the nineteenth century that awakens a sense of the mystery of her love for everyone, both friend and foe alike. Her deep love of God, and the shameful way in which she was treated, shows the light of Christ shining through her sheer goodness, making her more than human. Her acquaintance with many forms of suffering invites people to pray to the Sacred Heart through her.

Mary MacKillop was born on 15 January 1842 at Brunswick Street, Fitzroy, or, as it used to be known, Newtown, Melbourne. Her parents, Alexander MacKillop and Flora MacDonald, were immigrants from the Scottish Highlands, the Braes of Lochaber, near Inverness, described as the cradle of Catholicism in Scotland.

Alexander had trained for the priesthood but was never ordained.[5] He was the first member of his immediate family to come to Australia in 1838, on board *The Brilliant*. He was twenty-six. Alexander and Flora met in Melbourne in 1840. After what may well have been a whirlwind romance they were married on 14 July the same year.

Their first home was Marino Cottage, where Mary was born. She was the first Australian offshoot of this alliance that had its roots in the steep hillsides of Lochaber, which called for courage and endurance. She was the eldest of eight children. Margaret (Maggie) was the second and their third child was John. He was followed by Alick, who died when he was only eleven months, then there were Annie, Lexie (Alexandrina), Donald and finally Peter.

The period between the births of Mary and Maggie was the happiest time for the MacKillops. They owned a home of their own, and Alexander was employed with Campbell and Sons, a trading company, and had made good since coming to Melbourne. Unfortunately in 1841 he became involved with a syndicate, called 'The Apostles', whose aim was to rescue a pioneer trader who owed £10,000 to a bank. Alexander lost all his money and was declared bankrupt. He was not prudent where money was concerned, as this shows. He never recovered from the loss and was unable to provide adequately for his family. Mary and her younger brothers and sisters grew up in respectable poverty, dependent on the help of relatives.

Her mother was a devout person who taught Mary to trust in God and his providence. Mary wrote to her mother:

> It was in hardships, poverty and even want that you had to rear your children, but in the bitterest trial and greatest need your confidence in Divine Providence never failed.[6]

From a young age Mary was well aware of the worry of not having adequate food and clothing and at times not even a roof over their heads.

Her father was the teacher who did most for her education, especially in relation to religion and the Church. He enabled her to see the importance of education. She was very intelligent. Her letters are enlightening and full of spiritual encouragement. She wrote mainly to the Sisters of St Joseph and to her mother.

As the eldest of the family, Mary had a lot of responsibility. The weight of caring for the family fell on her. From her earliest days Mary was a nomad. Her family had no settled home of their own. The lack of their own home, the inability of their father to provide for them, the uncertainty of not knowing where they would be living, must have given rise to tensions, even quarrels, between her parents. Later, Mary was to write of her childhood with feelings of sadness:

> My life as a child was one of sorrows, my home when I had it, a most unhappy one.[7]

She was a very good horsewoman. She was able to handle horses skilfully and showed courage in controlling them. It was part of her character not to give in or to be beaten by anything but she had a love for animals.

Even in her childhood one can see evidence of her being prepared for the difficulties in her later life. Throughout her life she never shirked a hardship. When she was still a child she came home one day to find the baby Donald's nurse drunk. She dismissed her at once and looked after the baby herself. When she was a Sister in Adelaide she did prison visiting. She went to a murderer called

Fagan. She was warned not to go into his cell. She did; and he prayed with her, much to the amazement of the prison staff.

When she was eighteen (1860), and governess to her cousins at Penola in South Australia, she met someone who was to change her life. The parish priest at Penola was Father Julian Tenison Woods. His parish covered hundreds of square miles. He was often away for days at a time. He met many poor children who were running wild receiving no education. He wanted to start a new Religious Order to teach poor children. It would be a radical Order whose members would live with the people and move with them. They would be available to help them and to teach their children. He had come across the Sisters of St Joseph at Le Puy,[8] in France, when he was with the Marists. They were sent out to be with poor people. He wanted his Order to be modelled on them but it would be entirely new in Australia, where Religious life was thought of as living securely behind convent walls, as it was in Ireland. Together, they dreamt of taking Catholic education to poor children living in remote parts of the bush where there was no school, or at least none to which their parents could have afforded to send them.

Mary knew that she wanted to become a nun and to teach poor children. She had already decided that she did not want to join any of the existing Orders, like the Sisters of Mercy, who lived in cloisters and who had Choir and Lay Sisters. If she joined them she would only be able to teach those who could afford to pay. She would not be able to teach poor children to whom her heart reached out. She was adamant that she did not want any distinctions. All the Sisters were to be equal, as they were before God. At a time when rank, status and social position in the colonies mattered so much, Mary's conception of an Institute where none of these things mattered, was forward-looking, even revolutionary. No dowry was asked for or expected. It was the God-given meeting of two people who had the same dream.

In 1867 Mary opened the first Josephite school in a stable at Penola. It was a humble beginning, as it was for Jesus at Bethlehem. Bishop Sheil[9] visited the school, calling her Sister Mary, as though approving of the new Institute Father Woods and she were founding.

In the same year, Mary and Rose Cunningham came to Adelaide. Mary took her Vows and became the first Sister of St Joseph in Australia. Her religious name was Mary of the Cross MacKillop. It was prophetic. Her life was to be a multiplicity of crosses; *a nest of crosses* was how Julian Tenison Woods described her life. It was also one continuous prayer. She was always aware of the presence of God hidden in the ordinary things of life. She knew that she was called to bear her cross. She wrote to her mother, Flora:

> The Cross is my portion. It is also my sweet rest and support. I could not be happy without my cross. I would not lay it down for all the world could give. With the Cross I am happy but without it would be lost.[10]

Mary MacKillop lived by the power of the Cross, in the light of resurrection. She carried her cross without complaint, as a gift from God. She never shirked hardship because she saw it as Christ asking her to do something for him.

Father Woods drafted the First Rule for the new Institute. It gave prominence to no ownership. The Sisters would not own any property or material possessions and would live a life of poverty from contributions to the schools, as people could afford, or from alms. The Institute would have Central Government, which meant that, although the Sisters would work in various dioceses, they would not be under the control of the bishops but answerable to the Superior General of the Institute.

Mary of the Cross lived with three novices in Adelaide. They were the first community of nuns living in a small house in the city. They were innovators, or pioneers, and their lifestyle was simple and rudimentary. Above all they were free to go where they were needed.

They took charge of the Francis Xavier Cathedral Hall school, which had sixty students. The mother of the grandson of Governor Daly wished him to attend, provided he could receive special treatment, such as being kept separate from the other pupils. Mary would not have him in the school on these terms, which went against her principle of equal treatment for all.

By 1869, more than half the Catholic schools in Adelaide – seventeen in all – were run by the Sisters. There were thirty-eight Sisters and thirty-two novices. From then on, schools were set up round Adelaide and in other parts of South Australia.

There was another development in 1869. Mary was asked by Bishop James Quinn in Queensland to bring some Sisters to set up Josephite schools. They stayed in Queensland until 1879, when Mary was obliged to withdraw them after trouble with the Bishop, who wanted control over the Sisters. However, Mary would not yield to his demands. He called her 'an ambitious, obstinate woman, a disobedient nun, and a very troublesome woman'.[11]

Bishop Matthew Quinn,[12] brother of James Quinn, asked Mary to establish a community in Bathurst, New South Wales, in 1871. Mary took a group of Sisters from Adelaide. The Bishop of Bathurst turned out to be particularly antagonistic to Central Government. Mary resisted his attempts. He tried to change their Rule so that he had power over what they taught. He succeeded in getting a group of young women under his control. They were mainly postulants he had brought to his diocese from Ireland. Mary wisely let the Sisters choose whether they would return to Adelaide or stay with the Bishop. All except one Sister remained faithful to their Rule: Sister Hyacinth stayed to train the postulants at the urgent request of Bishop Quinn.

Mary returned to Adelaide in April 1871. While she had been away, things had not been going smoothly for the Sisters in Adelaide, some of whom claimed to have had visionary experiences. They managed to impress Father Woods with their accounts and had been encouraged by him. He regarded them as being very saintly. Mary was more cautious and believed the visions were delusions, and that Father Woods had been imprudent in giving them his support. This, however, was only part of the trouble.

Mary had foreseen potential problems with regard to Father Woods relations with other priests in the diocese.

He had become Director General of Catholic Education and Inspector of Schools in South Australia. He was unpopular. Dislike of him focused on the Sisters too. Many rumours were circulating among the priests about the Sisters, who were being made the objects of ridicule and were charged with being incompetent teachers, which was far from being the case. Bishop Sheil's health was declining and he was so influenced by what he heard about the Sisters from the priests that he excommunicated Sister Mary in the chapel at Franklin Street, and dispersed the Adelaide Sisters. Mary wrote:

> The sensation of the calm beautiful presence of God I shall never forget[13]

Owning no house, they had nowhere to go, but they had friends in their time of need. Emmanuel Solomon, a Jew, provided a house for the Sisters to live in. Joanna and Robert Barr Smith, Anglicans, were supportive. Jesuit priests at Norwood Church, Adelaide, stood by Mary and tended to her needs. This very tragic mistake was put right within a few months, just before Bishop Sheil died. It is hard for us to imagine what the experience of excommunication would have been like for Mary MacKillop and the Sisters. It must have been like being shipwrecked. Restitution would have been justified vindication for the Sisters.

In order to set matters straight regarding the Rule and Central Government, Mary went to Rome in 1873. She travelled as a lay person, to have the Rule approved. It took Rome two years to approve the Constitutions after they had changed the tenet of no ownership to owning property. In particular they were to own a Mother House in Adelaide. Even with the sanction of Rome, the bishops still tried to get control. Sadly, Father Woods was upset that Mary had gone to Rome without seeing him first, although she had tried unsuccessfully. He was very much against the decision of Rome to make owning property mandatory. He believed that

Mary should have defended no ownership which she did not do. It was a very hard time for Mary. It was the end of their working together.

Her sense of the Will of God and the hand of God in everything is what gave her the courage to face daunting tasks. Speaking about the Institute, she wrote to the Sisters:

> God will protect His own work. Never is he nearer to it than when danger threatens.[14]

This shows her very real sense of God being at work in our lives. God was not some remote father figure for her. God was more of a landscape gardener, creating pathways in our lives.

She returned to Adelaide at the beginning of 1875, having visited Scotland and Ireland and been on a pilgrimage to Paray-le-Monial, in France, while Rome was considering the Rule. Back in Adelaide, she was elected Superior General of the Institute. In the same year she went back to Queensland, taking with her the Constitutions that had been approved by Rome. She went for the sole purpose of trying to come to terms with Bishop James Quinn. There was no possibility of a compromise. He wanted control of the Sisters. She had no choice but to withdraw them from Queensland.

Mary brought the Sisters from Queensland to Sydney. She had the support of Archbishop Vaughan[15] who did not interfere with the Constitutions. Mary spoke of him as being 'more than kind'. They established schools and a Providence house for destitute women and children. They set up an orphanage for boys at Kincumber and an orphanage for girls at Lane Cove. Once again, God had led them to fresh pastures and many more needy children. In 1883 Mother Mary settled in Mount Street, North Sydney. The property was a gift from Dean Kenny.[16] She wrote from there:

> We have no noise, bustle or excitement. There is a nice little garden, a paddock with a high fence and birds singing around us.[17]

She was happy there and frequently wrote of how well she was when she was in Sydney.

Bishop Sheil was succeeded by Bishop Reynolds[18] who, at first, was very well-disposed to the Josephites, but, with the animosity of the priests towards the Sisters, he became disaffected. He decided to set up a Commission in 1883 to inquire into the affairs of the Sisters of St Joseph in South Australia.

They were in debt over the Mother House at Kensington but more serious was the accusation of alcoholism, which originated in Mary taking brandy as a medicinally-prescribed remedy for her health problems. She had a condition known as dysmenorrhea[19] which gave her a lot of pain. Brandy was the only known remedy. It was a very bitter time for Mary. Not all the Sisters were as loyal and truthful as they should have been. The matter ended quite tragically. Mary was expelled from Adelaide without being allowed to give any reason to the Sisters for her departure. This led to misunderstanding, grief and, in some cases, a feeling of being abandoned by the Mother they loved. Some Sisters left Adelaide and went to Sydney. On a more cheerful note, the first New Zealand foundation was begun in Temuka in 1883.

Mary was re-elected as Superior General at the second Chapter in 1881 but she herself doubted that her election was valid. That term of office came to an abrupt end when Sister Bernard was appointed Superior General in 1885, and Mary faced the tragedy of her beloved mother's death in May 1886. Flora was drowned when *The Ly-ee-Moon* sank off the coast of Green Cape, near Eden, New South Wales.

The expansion of the Institute continued with the first foundation in Victoria in 1889 at Numurkah. This was followed by a school at Bacchus Marsh. In 1890 a Children's Home was started at Surrey Hills, a suburb of Melbourne. Archbishop Carr asked Mother Mary to come and help. This was what the Sisters of St Joseph had been founded for – to serve Christ in his 'neglected little ones'. But Victoria was in the midst of a financial crisis and money was in short supply, especially for a children's home. Mother Mary referred to herself as 'Beggar-in-Chief'. In

1892, she became seriously ill and was thought to be dying. According to the doctor, it was only prayer that saved her.

In time, she was well enough to travel again and began a series of visits to New Zealand, a country she loved. Her first was in 1894–5, the second from 1897–8, the third in 1900 and the last one in 1902. Her first time consisted of arduously travelling from North to South Island and back again, stopping at all the Josephite convents. Her second visit was cut short because of the news of Mother Bernard's unexpected death. Mary returned to Sydney at once, and was elected Superior General at the Fifth Chapter in 1899. When she returned for her third visit she knew her responsibilities as Superior General would not allow her to be away from Australia for long, but there were matters in New Zealand that needed her attention. Her fourth visit was under doctor's orders to go to the medicinal baths at Rotorua, for a cure for her arthritis. She had been there four months when she had a stroke. Her right side was paralysed and she was confined to a wheelchair. She returned to Sydney at the end of 1902.

In 1904 she made a journey to Victoria and South Australia. It was her last journey to see her Sisters there. She continued to make decisions regarding the Institute. She still had to endure physical pain, which she described as a toothache in every part of her body.

Mary of the Cross was beginning to struggle with governing the Congregation from her wheelchair. She gradually grew weaker. In August 1909, having not spoken for some days, she was asked if she would like the Blessed Sacrament and answered clearly that she would. She never spoke again. Father Matthew Smith went to the oratory for the Blessed Sacrament and when he returned he found the way to her room strewn with flower petals that had fallen from a vase. The beauty and fragility of the petals spoke of the beauty of the self-giving vulnerability of the woman who was dying within.

She is buried in the chapel at Mount Street, North Sydney, which has become a shrine of pilgrimage. There is nothing more peaceful one can do than go and kneel beside her tomb, which has her words engraved on it: *Remember we are but travellers here* and

*Trust in God*. Blessed Mary MacKillop is still very much alive today. So many people carry her in their hearts.

Mary MacKillop was beatified in Sydney on 19 January 1995, by Pope John Paul II. She was a woman of vision. People have said that she was a woman before her time. But her vision was so relevant and necessary for the hard times in which she lived that one can only say she was a desperately-needed woman for her times, when poor children were not being educated or cared for. The education of poor children, whose parents could not afford to send them to a school, and many of whom were living in ignorance of their faith, was the firm foundation of her vision. Everything else that caused her so much trouble came about through putting her vision into practice. To some extent it was the old, old story of men who could not tolerate a woman speaking her mind, no matter how courteously she did it. They could not understand or accept the idea of Religious life for women being lived in the bush, on the gold fields, outside the jurisdiction of bishops, wherever there was a need. It was a thicket of crosses that Mary was caught in, without any complaint or rancour.

Many of her obituary notices are headed 'Mother Mary of the Cross', as though proclaiming the heavy cross she had carried throughout her life. She endured what might be described as a 'tsunami' of opposition from one bishop after another, and from many priests, especially those in South Australia.

She lived her spirituality of trusting God. She walked with sure feet on the rugged mountains of God's challenges to her.

# 2

# Mary MacKillop and the Will of God

## Introduction

Mary MacKillop did not leave any systematic writings for posterity, although some of her letters,[1] *Circulars* to the Sisters,[2] and some of her addresses,[3] have been published. From these documents, it is evident that the Will of God was central to her theology. I am using the term 'theology' to refer to a person's beliefs about God which influence how he or she lives, as well as how he or she thinks. Mary MacKillop had no dry, academic thoughts, and she was remarkably free from limiting conventionalism – so much so that she has been referred to as 'a woman before her time'.[4]

Her busy and often troubled life was filled with a supreme sense of God. Writing around 1924, just fifteen years after Mary Mac-Killop's death, Evelyn Underhill maintained that 'enrichment of the sense of God is the crying need of our current Christianity,'[5] words that are no less true today. Mary MacKillop had a very rich sense of the presence of God in her life. She had a sense of her life going somewhere, and of things over which she had no control happening for a purpose, which she might not always understand. She accepted this as the Will of God. In this paper I shall argue that her devotion to the Will of God was what created the story of the Sisters of St Joseph and her own story as their founder.

It is only when we try to understand the nature of Mary MacKillop's passionate love for the Will of God that we can begin to appreciate why she has recently been acclaimed 'a saint for Australia'. Her generosity of spirit and sense of justice were firmly rooted in her understanding of the Will of God. Thus, to think of her as battling for the underdog or as providing 'a lesson in resistance'[6] without taking into account her theology of the Will of God, is to lose sight altogether of the heart of her faith, from which her deep concern for the social evils of the times welled up.

In this chapter, I shall explore the salient features of Mary MacKillop's theology of the Will of God in three stages: the creativity of her approach, that connected the will and the Person of God, her view of the association between the will and the Word of God, and the relation between her will and the divine will. At each stage a particular question will be dealt with; in the first: how did Mary MacKillop understand the Will of God?; in the second: how did she know the Will of God?; and, in the third: how did she do the Will of God?

## Mary MacKillop's creative approach to the Will of God

How did Mary MacKillop understand the Will of God? Unfortunately, she did not write any treatise on the subject but we can be certain that she did not think of it as we do today. Her approach to the Will of God was to some extent conditioned by nineteenth-century spirituality, which differs from the twenty-first-century approach. It is probably the case that we tend to think of the Will of God in terms of God's plan for our lives. A plan is something rational, and we can feel comfortable with that. When she spoke of God's Will as being 'adorable',[7] Mary MacKillop was clearly not thinking of a blueprint, but of something by which she felt herself to be overwhelmed. The terminology of abandonment that she used to describe her response to God's Will is also alien to our modern way of thinking, that has resulted from our theological 'coming of age'.[8] Consequently, we do not feel at home with concepts such as 'resignation', 'surrender' and 'abandonment' in relation to God's Will that seem to nullify our human wills. But these terms were idiomatic in nineteenth-century Australian spirituality, which was strongly influenced by French spirituality.[9] Although we must beware of imposing our twenty-first-century culture and idioms upon Mary MacKillop's thought, we need to reclaim the creativity of her theology of the Person and Will of God from the cultural milieu of her day, so as to find its relevance for us in the twenty-first century.

When she spoke of the Will of God, it was always in a personal way, as 'her haven in the storm and trials which beset her on all sides'.[10] We do not always think of the Will of God as a haven in times of stress. It is more often the case that people speak about the Will of God impersonally, in relation to death or some other unwelcome event, implying almost fatalistically that this is how things have to be. Thus, God's Will is thought of as being juxtaposed to the individual's will or at least indifferent to it. A similar de-personalisation of the Will of God occurs when someone says 'It is God's Will' as an excuse for human failure to prevent a wrong, or put right something that is wrong. An explanation of the view that God's Will is an intrusion into our affairs is that we find it difficult to reconcile God-the-omnipotent-creator with God-the-all-loving-Father (or -Mother). We find it hard to integrate the different aspects of power and love in the divine nature. And, with regard to God's Will, there is a tendency to align it with the power aspect rather than with God's love, and consequently we are inclined to be fearful of its demands. There were no such divisions in Mary MacKillop's thought of the divine nature. For her, Love is all-powerful and Power is Love in action. Her unified thought of God's Personhood was a significant factor in how she thought about the Will of God.

Daniel Lyne brings out her personal and creative approach to the Will of God when he talks about the way in which she connected the Will of God with his Person:

> She did not see this Will of God as an impersonal force. It is interesting in her letters to see how she 'personalises' the concept of the Will of God. Even within one letter she moves from speaking about the 'Will of God' to speaking about the 'person of God', as though they are, for her, the same thing. (*Mary MacKillop, Made in Australia* p33)

In a sense, the Will of God must be connected with his Person because the will essentially belongs to personhood. It is a fundamental characteristic of persons that they have the capacity to make decisions and to act upon them. We ascribe these powers to the will. Since persons are made in the image of God, the Will of God is integral to the Person of God. By saying that Mary

MacKillop identified the Will of God with the Person of God, Daniel Lyne is stressing that for her the Will of God was never impersonal like the force of gravity, of Fate, or a dictatorial super-will. Such a view was alien to her thinking because it treated the Will of God as an external power, being imposed on a person's will. Although she sometimes spoke about 'submitting'[11] to God's Will, as though she had no will of her own, this was always a response to what she felt to be a personal call to love, rather than to something that was imposed upon her.

Her attitude to the divine will was both positive and creative, and resulted from what Daniel Lyne refers to as her ability to 'personalise' the Will of God. To talk about 'personalising' God's Will is ambiguous. In one sense, to 'personalise' the Will of God is to regard it as issuing from the Person of God, whose love for each one of us is changeless. And, in another sense, it is to make God's Will personal to oneself. Mary MacKillop 'personalised' the Will of God in both senses. Thus, she always thought of God's Will as divine love in action; and as issuing from an overflowing of His love for us. But, more importantly, she saw God's Will as a creative force within her own life, giving shape to her life, as intimately as a potter shapes the clay into a vessel. She did not consider the possibility of God's Will frustrating her will. Instead she feared doing her own will in preference to God's, lest by doing so she was hindering the hand of the Master craftsman at work in her own life. Even though she used terms such as 'resignation', 'subservience', 'acceptance' and 'abandonment' to describe her attitude to the Will of God, their meaning is joyfully expansive, because they express her willing co-operation with the divine artist whose work of art she believed herself to be. Thus, she was able to speak of 'the beautiful, wise Will of God' (Letter 5 March 1870) because God's creative power had overall priority in her life. The central importance she gave to the Will of God is also brought out in her description of God's Will as 'the lodestar',[12] shining in the depths of her being, rimming her life with its light.

The Will of God was *the* formative influence in her being, to which she joyfully yielded herself, body, mind and spirit. But there was nothing weak or passive about her attitude. She had a rich sense of the Will of God at work in the circumstances, events and persons of her life. When troubles came, as they did in plenty, she looked at them creatively to find concealed in them the Will of God for her at the particular time and in the particular circumstances in which she found herself. This meant that she deliberately removed 'the devices and desires' of her own will, to allow the Will of God to flow freely through her into the situations in her own life and the lives of others.

Mary knew in a costly way that the Will of God was to be accepted, and she also gave advice to others whom she believed to be resisting the Will of God on some matter. In doing so, we see her again giving a very personal view of the divine will. In the letter to which Daniel Lyne is referring in the above quotation, she writes of the Will of God 'laughing' when someone is resisting, and goes on to describe such a person as 'a helpless infant'.[13] To talk about the Will of God as laughing is a quaint personification but by using the image of a loving father, laughing at his child who is vainly struggling to go his own way, she succeeds in presenting God's Will in a totally non-threatening way. It is a picture that is also evoked by the words of Psalm 139:

> 'You hem me in, behind and before, and lay your hand upon me.' (Ps. 139:5)

They conjure up the image of a human father (or mother) who is shielding his or her child from any possible harm. Mary MacKillop could simply have pointed out that God's Will is sovereign and that it is pointless to resist; but instead she dwells upon the loving, humanly irresistible, person of God, who plays with us, not capriciously, but with intimate concern for our well-being. The imagery she uses, of play, laughter and parenting, is similar to contemporary views of the divine nature such as the image of a divine Dancer who leads us in a creative dance, used by Thomas Merton[14] and Sidney Carter. Such imagery changes our understanding of God's Will from being oppressively demanding to being creative, and humanly attractive, inviting us to partnership.

Far from being an external force impinging upon her life, the Will of God was rooted in Mary MacKillop's spiritual make-up. It was a lens through which she could make sense of whatever happened in her life. The difficulties that she encountered were never just adverse circumstances; they were the new shape of what a loving God was bringing into being. To be able to view events that threatened the well-being of the Sisters, and even her own Religious life, as issuing from the Will of God, or at least from God's permissive will, called for what Jean Pierre de Caussade called 'the instinct of faith'. I quote:

> It (the instinct of faith) lives in God and his works even when they seem harmful ...[15]

To have the instinct of faith, however, does not mean that a person is never daunted by circumstances. Like anybody else, Mary MacKilllop had her moments of human weakness, as we can see from the letter she wrote to Julian Tenison Woods at the time of her wrongful excommunication:

> I think I should have fled before this for, as each week brought something fresh in the 'Harp', I felt so tempted to go and never let you and anyone else know where I went. (November 1871)

At a time of great trial, when she was understandably at the end of her tether, it was her 'instinct of faith' that kept her holding fast to her trust that the 'beautiful wise' Will of God would prevail. Three years later, she wrote:

> God kept my heart full of trust to make all come right. (30 October 1874)

A more recent approach to the Will of God is that of Simone Weil, who likens the difference between pain and happiness to ink of two different colours.[16] What matters is not the colour of the ink but the message written in it. Thus, the love and Will of God are just as present in the difficulties that cause us pain as in the events that bring us joy. Mary MacKillop took the same creative, positive attitude to the Will of God as Simone Weil. We can see this in the following extract from a letter she wrote on Ascension Day 1873 to Monsignor Kirby:

> I can never pray for a particular intention, a particular person, or anything particular about the Institute, but in God's loved will … Thus, I feel a joy when things go wrong or against our natural desire, for there again I see His will …

The Will of God for Mary MacKillop was a matter of trusting that 'all things work together for good' (Rom. 8:28). But it was more than that; it was the key to understanding everything that happened in her life. It was a story that she owned as hers and God's, and the colour of the ink in which it was written did not matter.

## The Will and the Word of God in Mary MacKillop's Theology

It is natural to connect the will with words. We generally know the will of another by what he or she says. Mary MacKillop's single-mindedness with regard to the Will of God was rooted in the Word of God. Volume III of the *Positio, Informatio de Virtutibus*[17] begins with these words:

> The whole of Mary MacKillop's long life was a response to God's Word spoken in her heart at an early age, a Word that grew ever more demanding. Her personal virtue, all the works she took up, her tireless activity, were an expression of her concern to be faithful to that Word.

These remarks leave no doubt that she knew the Will of God in a direct and powerful way from a young age. We do not know what particular words God spoke in her heart but they kindled a desire in her to be and do as God willed. In this sense, the Word of God, the Logos, was very personal to her; and it was a formative influence in her life. It would be a mistake to suppose that she thought of God's Will merely as a plan for her life. The Logos in her heart was more like a writer's inspiration for a story that had yet to be told.

It is sometimes the case that words of Scripture can come to mean a great deal in a person's life. For many years the prophet Isaiah's words, 'Make straight in the desert a highway for your God,' were a beacon in my life. And it was both a confirming experience and the end of a very personal story when I heard His Holiness, Pope John Paul II, speaking about them in his homily at the Beatification of Blessed Mary MacKillop.

It may not only be words that have this personal significance in someone's life. In his autobiography, *The Story and the Fable*, the Scottish poet, Edwin Muir, explains how he assessed his life and set himself tasks in the light of a recurring and significant image – a shaft of sunlight shining through particles of dust that rise up to meet it. It became a symbol and a personal focus of meaning and value in his life. Similarly, for Mary MacKillop, the Word of God that she held in the depths of her heart became the touchstone of everything that mattered to her. She was alert to it and by this Word she steered her life, set her short and long term goals, and undertook the many duties of her young and adult life. She would have drawn little, if any, distinction between the Word and the Will of God as she knew them in the depths of her being.

Another way in which it might be helpful to think of the significance of the Word and the Will of God in a person's life is in terms of the Aboriginal idea of dreaming, which is central to their spirituality. The Aboriginal idea of dreaming is rich and complex and I cannot do justice to it in the limited scope of this chapter; but it can throw light on the way that the Will of God creates or forms the flow of significant events in someone's life, which is how I believe the Will of God guided Mary MacKillop and her Institute. Dreaming, in Aboriginal culture, is connected with other concepts such as story, myth, sagas and history. It is a concept that links the spiritual world beyond time with what is happening in time; it covers all departments of the socio-spiritual realm, including education, art, law, artefacts and the land, in all its different aspects, such as landscape, sacred sites and geographical features. Anything which changes the Aboriginal way of life is explained as part of the dreaming. The nurturing Word in Mary MacKillop's heart similarly brought the Will of God into every department of her life, bestowing value and significance. It was the matrix from which the story of both founder and Institute unfolded. But whereas Aboriginal dreaming is a socio-spiritual idea that explains the structures of Aboriginal society, for Mary MacKillop, the Will of God was also very personal, as we have seen. What I am suggesting is that, just as the dreaming is connected with the story of a people, so the Will of God was the spiritual source in the hearts of Mary MacKillop and her Sisters from which the Josephite story has flowed into the structures and spirituality of Australian society.

What was particularly distinctive about the Institute of the Sisters of St Joseph arose from the vision or dreaming of its two founders, Julian Tenison Woods and Mary MacKillop. Their dreaming, which began independently, was initially a compassionate awareness of the desperate social need of children of the poorest families, living in remote areas of the bush, to receive an education. The times were dangerous; Ned Kelly and plenty of other criminal types were at large, roads were rough and the bush largely untamed. But the Sisters were to go forth to the people, because it was the Will of God, so placing the mission of the Institute above and beyond social work and making it an apostolic instrument for the doing of God's Will. But if Mary MacKillop had not cherished the Word given to her by God at the beginning, the pioneering story of the Sisterhood might never have taken root in the history of Australia.

As well as the Word of God, spoken within a person's heart, there is the Logos in the written word of Scripture. However, our present-day approach to the Bible is very different to that of Mary MacKillop's time. We live in an age of *midrash*, when Scripture is open to different interpretations and biblical texts are freely discussed. Although Christian scholarship regards the Bible as the living Word of God, it is also the case that the words of Scripture are sifted intellectually for possible meanings. Mary MacKillop's approach was devotional, and there is little evidence to lead one to suppose that she was a biblical scholar. The fact that she rarely used texts from Scripture in her writings suggests that it was not the words themselves that mattered to her so much as the persons the Scriptures spoke about – the Virgin Mary, Joseph, Jesus and John the Baptist, whose lives instantiated the Will of God. In her meditations based on Our Lord's Passion,[18] she employed the contemplative method of St Ignatius. Thus, she entered with imagination and feeling into the portrayal of persons and situations in the Gospel story and ascertained the Will of God for herself and the Institute she co-founded, drawing upon these New Testament models.

The Virgin Mary's response, 'Be it done unto me according to your will,' expressing her single-mindedness to collaborate with Creative Love, whatever the consequences, would have resonated strongly in Mary MacKillop's heart, because it was the beginning of a story initiated by God in partnership with a simple country girl, who became the willing centrepiece of the story. Her choice of the patrons of the Institute, Joseph, Jesus and John the Baptist, was grounded on the respective selfless circumstances of their lives. She had a special devotion to Joseph, guardian of Mary and Jesus and of the Institute, and in her meditation on 'The Virtues of Our Holy Patron'[19] she praises his humble and hidden life that collaborated with the Will of God in the story of redemption. Thus, in the Gospel she saw the Will of God at work in the lives of little people who allowed themselves to be caught up in God's great story of salvation. Just as the Word was made flesh in the lives of Mary and Joseph by their acceptance of the Will of God beyond all reason, so through the Sisters of St Joseph the Word made flesh could become a reality in the lives of Australians who had fallen on hard times and were falling away from their Catholic faith.

In his book, *Mary MacKillop, Spirituality and Charisms*, Daniel Lyne discusses the nature of the special charism of the founder of an institute.[20] He points out that since Vatican II, an important dimension of the founder's charism is his or her reading of the Gospel, 'which tends to highlight some aspect of the life of Jesus, which, when applied in mission, forms a compelling new vision and way of life'. Although Mary MacKillop was living and working about a hundred years before Vatican II, it is relevant in its light to see how Scripture – in particular the life of Jesus – impinged upon her theology of the Will of God, and how it gave rise to a 'compelling new vision' and to the charisms of the Institute of the Sisters of St Joseph. What makes Mary MacKillop's vision compelling is its resonance with particular aspects of the Gospel. However, it does not seem to matter whether the compelling nature of the vision is directly the result of the founder's reading of the Gospel or not. The fact that the Sisters of St Joseph followed so closely in the footsteps of Jesus in order to serve the poor has been found compelling by others.

Jesus' story, as we read about it in the Gospels, was of a journey or series of journeys,[21] which were a continual moving out to be with the people. He was unencumbered by property, undeterred by convention and never deflected from his mission by opposition from the establishment. This compassionate mobility of Jesus, who tabernacled with us to do the Will of God, and who belonged to an ancient tradition of wandering, desert folk whose desert story was lived, at least in remembrance, is a compelling factor in the authenticity of the Josephite mission. The Sisters of St Joseph were to embody these charisms[22] by bringing to birth a new type of 'desert' women religious in the early days of the colony. They lived in twos and threes, outside convent walls, moved from place to place with the people, taught the children and took the Word of God to those beyond reach of the Church, despite difficulties and opposition to the idea of nomadic nuns from Catholic bishops and priests, because that was the vision of the Will of God with respect to the mission of the Institute, given to the founders, Mary MacKillop and Julian Tenison Woods.

The Institute of the Sisters of St Joseph of the Sacred Heart was founded, first and foremost, on an understanding of the Will of God with regard to those who had been called into that particular Institute. In a meditation, 'For the Last Day of St Joseph's Month',[23] Mary MacKillop set down for her Sisters the *raison d'être* of the Institute:

We are here in religion, and the work we have to do is to let the Will of God be accomplished in us by our becoming saints. We are not saints – far from it; but it is God's Will that we should become such, and it is to give us an opportunity of becoming such that He has mercifully called us into the Institute of which we are members ... He has called us to the Institute, and according to its rules and the spirit of them, does he need us to be saints.

She regarded the rules as the expression of the Will of God that directly affected the daily lives of the Sisters. In general terms, the reasons for the existence of the Institute are similar to those for the existence of any other institute, namely the sanctification of its members. However, a vocation to be a Sister of St Joseph was a call to a radical death to the world that was not required by other religious institutes of the time. There were no distinctions between whether they were rich or poor. Those entering the Institute were not required to bring a dowry. In the spirit of the Gospel they were to sacrifice themselves in the service of those who lived on the social margins.

It is salutary to realise, when there is earnest searching for the Will of God today, with regard to the future of Religious life,[24] that the Institute Mary MacKillop and Julian Tenison Woods founded broke away from the traditional mould in order to answer the needs of the time. Just as Religious and others, at present, urge the need to find a right balance between mission or ministry and commitment to community, it is helpful to recognise that the founder of one of the largest Australian congregations saw clearly the importance of community nurturing the meaning of Religious life. However urgent their mission, it was not to be allowed to subtract from the expression of the Sisters' love of the Will of God in their consecrated life together. How else would they be able to continue to discern the Will of God in their daily circumstances and to have the strength to do it? Nevertheless, it is only when we understand the condition of those *to whom* the Sisters of St Joseph were sent that we can begin to realise the rugged, self-denying way in which they were called to work towards their sanctification.

In her description of a socially-deprived underclass that had developed in the early days of the Australian colony, Janet McCalman[25] refers to the nineteenth-century term 'residuum'. She writes:

> These were the people for whom the world of respectability and regular work had no place. This was the abyss of failure ...

To talk about 'the socially underprivileged' really conveys nothing of the humiliation and abject misery of victims of the 'residuum'. The 'residuum' can be compared with the condition of affliction about which Simone Weil has written so articulately in her description of French society in the 1940s. She writes:

> Affliction is like a device for pulverising the soul; the man who falls into it is like a workman who gets caught up in a machine. He is no longer a man but a torn and bloody rag on the teeth of a cog-wheel.[26]

Affliction has nothing to do with suffering, which can be a transforming influence in a person's life. Affliction is a dehumanising force that robs a person of all self-respect and injects the inertia of despair into the soul. According to Simone Weil, 'The world needs saints who have genius, just as a plague-stricken town needs doctors'.[27] The first Josephites lived their vocation in the midst of the 'residuum', in the same spirit as doctors who go to the aid of a plague-stricken city. As they permeated the structures of society, they became a new force for good in the lives of many people. And the story of the Institute became part of the story of the Australian people, whose lives rose again on wings of hope from the ashes of despair.

## Mary MacKillop's Spirituality of Doing the Will of God

For Mary MacKillop, doing God's Will was essentially concerned with a person's spiritual formation. Thus, I have deliberately used the term 'spirituality' rather than 'theology' in relation to doing the Will of God. Her main concern was with the practical matter of motives and *how* someone does the Will of God: for example, willingly, in readiness and obediently. She regarded the matter of how a person does the Will of God as being part of the very wellsprings of that person's spirituality. Her approach was via the concept of self-emptying (*kenosis*), which she saw as a prerequisite for doing the Will of God. She admonished her Sisters with the words 'Be generous with God'; in other words, they were not to question, reason why or hold back. Doing the Will of God generously demanded *kenosis*.

The idea of a person doing God's Will inevitably raises the question of how an individual agent's will is viewed in relation to the divine Will. Probably the commonest view is that if a person is doing God's Will, then he or she is not free to do his or her own will. Thus, doing God's Will tends to be thought of as imposing constraints upon a person. As we have seen, in describing her own will as she sought to do what she believed to be God's Will for her, Mary MacKillop used the 'in-words' of the times, such as 'resigned', 'subservient' and 'submissive'. This is the language of enslavement. To speak of an individual's will in terms that imply being enslaved to the Will of God could be taken, wrongly, as implying a totally passive attitude that denies personal autonomy. A slave has no freedom about what he or she does. When Mary MacKillop spoke in terms of being resigned to God's Will, she was certainly not renouncing her human capacity to make decisions. She was humbly setting aside her own preferences and immediate objectives in order to do the Will of God as it presented itself to her at a particular time. She would gladly have said that she wanted to serve God as a slave because that would have expressed the sense of self-emptying she felt to be necessary in order to do the Will of

God. However, although it was natural for her to use the vocabulary of servitude that was currently in vogue at the time, it did not adequately express her own positive sense of being called into something greater than herself when she did God's Will.

Her positive approach to doing the Will of God is evident in the Ascension Day letter she wrote to Monsignor Kirby, in which she said: 'I long to do the Will of God perfectly.' In saying this, she saw her own will as being active, full of potential for goodness. It would be a mistake, however, to suppose that her longing to do the Will of God perfectly was the expression of a desire for a mystical union with God's Will that would leave her no will of her own. Whenever Mary MacKillop spoke of union with God it was always 'spousal union', in which the identity and will of each party is retained. When she wrote 'I long to do the Will of God perfectly,' she was uttering the language of willing co-operation or collaboration. To collaborate with another is to do more than just to go along with their aims and objectives. It is actively to promote them.

How did Mary MacKillop understand the idea of collaborating with God's Will? Daniel Lyne uses the phrase 'making God's Will work for her'.[28] Although I doubt that she would ever have thought in terms of 'making' God's Will do anything, the sense of the phrase is that she chose to see God's Will at work on her behalf in everything. It is also the case that in order to make something work for one, it is necessary to understand it. Mary MacKillop understood the Will of God as being good through and through, even when she was being asked to do or to endure something that was hard for her. She saw the Will of God at such times as a mystery, through which she would have safe passage. She did the Will of God and urged the Sisters to do God's Will in such a way that it would be a springboard to faith.

It is helpful, in discussing what it is to do the Will of God, to employ metaphorical language, in order to grasp the relation between the human and divine wills. Mary MacKilllop herself employed a metaphor, from which we get some indication of how she understood what it is to do God's Will, when she spoke of herself doing the Will of God as an instrument,[29] which comes close to the more familiar idea nowadays of a person being used as a channel. As far as I know, Mary MacKillop did not refer to herself as a channel for God's Will, but there is little or no substantial difference between the two metaphors. Both an instrument and a channel are used as the means to further the user's end.

However, a channel is a more fertile illustration for our purposes because it lends itself to explaining what is involved in doing the Will of God. To be God's instrument is to be used by God to achieve God's purposes, whether one consciously intends this or not. A channel, on the other hand, needs to be intentionally kept open so that water can flow through it freely. In order to be a channel, a person may have to clear away mental obstacles (self-emptying) that could be blocking the flow of God's love. Being an effective channel for the Will of God to be done would mean that there was nothing of self-will to impede the out-flowing of God's love to those who need to receive it. Such obstacles include self-centred attitudes such as wilfulness, unwillingness and self-importance, which operate at what might be described meta-phorically as the 'surface' level of volition, and may constitute a focus of self-preoccupation. When Mary MacKillop spoke about having no will of her own, she was deliberately renouncing her 'surface' will in self-emptying, and embracing a self-forgetful poverty of spirit with regard to it.

However, there is a deeper level of will, which is the well-spring of a person's life-structuring motives that connect with faith and give direction and overall purpose to a person's life. When the writer of Proverbs wrote 'Keep your heart with all vigilance, for from it flow the issues of life' (Prov. 4:23), he was referring to motives that both direct and govern the will and also shape a person's identity. It is at the formative level of the will that the motive to become a channel for God's Will wells up. But there may be tension between the two levels of volition. When Mary MacKillop wrote of her longing to do the Will of God perfectly, one thing she meant was that she longed for this life-structuring motive to flush out whatever she feared might impede the flow of

God's loving Will at the 'surface' level of her will, causing her to do God's Will with less than total generosity. When she urged her Sisters to 'be generous with God,' she was advising them to allow their spirituality to be formed at its source by the longing to do the Will of God; and then to do God's Will wholeheartedly and single-mindedly without counting the cost.

In this final section on Mary MacKillop's spirituality of doing the Will of God, I have taken the line that we should not allow her use of the vocabulary of servitude to stand in the way of trying to understand what she meant when she spoke about having resigned her own will. Nor should we dismiss her longing to do God's Will perfectly as vague or too idealistic. Her own generosity towards doing God's Will is the key to understanding the distinctive quality of her holiness.

My aim throughout this chapter has been to present Mary MacKillop's devotion to the Will of God as *the* creative force in the story of her life and that of the Institute she founded with Julian Tenison Woods. Through her understanding of the Will of God, she presents us with a threefold challenge today: 1) to re-think our concept of God so that God's Will is seen as an intimate, formative source in our lives; 2) to see our own 'stories', and the meaning we give to our lives, as issuing from the Will of God, so that they each become a story of divine/human co-operation in the furthering of God's Kingdom among us; and 3) to recognise *how* we do God's Will as a criterion in our own spiritual development. All this would suggest that we need to revisit our theology of the Will of God.

# 3

## *Living Creatively with the Will of God — Mary MacKillop and Evelyn Underhill*

*The whole of Christian history really turns upon the power of human hope: this absolute hold upon the reality of God, His supernatural energy and freedom, with the corresponding conviction that He does and will act within the human arena, intervene to save. 'I am not a God afar off: I am thy Maker and friend' — a Maker who has not finished His work, but is making us all the time, whose capacity for loving action is inexhaustible.*

Evelyn Underhill

The Will of God is not the most usual way of talking about God today. We tend to think of the whole Person of God — God the loving Father or Mother, or, as Jesus taught, the intimate *Abba* God who knows each of us through and through. Why did theologians want to speak about God's Will rather than God's heart or mind? To single out the Will of God emphasises two aspects of God.

Firstly, that God's transcendent sovereignty is over everything. Theology of the Will of God is connected with a verse in Isaiah:

> For as the heavens are higher than the earth, so are my ways higher than your ways and my thoughts than your thoughts.[1]

It is important to remember that God's ways are not our ways when we are living with the Will of God in our lives.

Secondly, that God's Will is expressed by God's agency or activity, bringing things about in our affairs. It is also associated with the idea of a person being available to be God's instrument or channel so that he or she can carry out God's Will. God being active in our affairs and a person being an instrument for God both imply living with the Will of God. It is having an experience of recognising God's Will and having a sense of God's presence as we follow our pathway each day.

Living with the Will of God means more than being conscious of the possibility of God's agency bringing things about in our lives, in events and circumstances or by word, written or spoken. It means being aware of the Will of God woven through each day so that we always have the question in our minds: 'Is this what God wants of me now?' When we talk about living with the Will of God, we are saying that the Will of God is a dynamic factor. It makes things happen. It brings about changes, but it may need our co-operation to be able to do so. Mary MacKillop knew what living with the Will of God meant. She knew that God needed space in our lives for his will to be effective and that God relied on our willing collaboration. What was it like for Mary MacKillop and Evelyn Underhill to live with the Will of God? I want to show that it was first and foremost a creative experience, but it was also costly for Mary MacKillop, as it was for Evelyn Underhill.

As I have already said,[2] Will of God theology is hard for us today. There is a whole glossary of terms associated with it that do not sit comfortably with us: *surrender, submission, abandonment, resignation* and *compliance*. Their passivity is foreign to the hyperactive, do-it-yourself, fast-lane culture of the twenty-first century. We do not easily give up our own agendas today, never mind totally forsaking our own wills. This might be all right for an enclosed order of nuns but not for people living in the real world.

I should like to re-visit the Will of God spirituality, with the help of Mary MacKillop and Evelyn Underhill, for I believe that they had a much more positive attitude to accepting and living with the Will of God than we have. Very often we think of the Will of God as a divine plan for our lives. We feel more at home with that and do not want to venture beyond our comfort zones. If we ask how we relate to the Will of God in our attitudes today, they are largely negative. We fear that the Will of God will ask too much of us and ask for what we do not want to give. We have much to learn from both Mary MacKillop and Evelyn Underhill.

## Living with the Will of God

Living with the Will of God is finding the Will of God in the ordinary, everyday circumstances of our lives. For example, it is interesting to discover what text or saying a person has displayed on their desk. It shows where their daily focus is. Julian Tenison Woods kept a text from Deuteronomy on his desk:

> I shall be with thee; the Lord himself will be with thee and not abandon thee.

He lived with the loving, companioning presence of God day by day.

Evelyn Underhill, an Anglican theologian and spiritual director, who lived just a little after Mary MacKillop (1875–1941), chose a saying from St Augustine to keep on her desk:

> I toss upon the waves but Thou dost steer, Thou who standeth at the helm of all things Thou hast made.

Evelyn Underhill lived with the guiding hand of God upon the tiller of her life, as she tossed upon the sometimes troubled waters of the day; and she knew she would have safe passage. The idea of God being in charge, steering a course, connects with the guiding and directing Will of God.

We can only speculate about the text or saying Mary MacKillop would have kept on her desk. She could well have chosen those words from St Augustine that were so attractive and helpful to Evelyn Underhill, for she wrote something that shows the same sentiment:

> My soul is in peace, though my body is tossed upon the stormy waves of a cold and selfish world.[3]

She was able to be at peace because she lived with the knowledge that God was at the helm of her boat. She had nothing to fear.

Both these outstanding women believed that the acceptance of the sovereign, overruling Will of God was the key to living a spiritual life. They had been born in very different circumstances. Evelyn Underhill was a Londoner; Mary MacKillop was an Australian. Evelyn Underhill had a university education but her spirituality has the same humility and simplicity as Mary Mac-Killop's. Evelyn Underhill was married but she had no children. Her married name was Stuart Moore. They were nurtured in different Christian traditions. Anglicanism, or, rather, Anglo-Catholicism,[4] was Evelyn Underhill's denomination, and Catholicism was Mary MacKillop's. Yet through their respective traditions they shared a common understanding of the importance of the Will of God.

Mary MacKillop learnt the wisdom of accepting the Will of God from her mother, Flora. Julian Tenison Woods used to write to her about obeying the Will of God and learning to have no will of one's own. It was an idea of renunciation derived from the fourteenth-century French spirituality of Thomas a Kempis, who wrote:

> ... he is most truly learned who doeth the Will of God and forsaketh his own will.[5]

The phrases 'having no will of one's own' and 'forsaking one's own will' belonged to the theological climate of the nineteenth century and were an important element in the popular devotion to the Sacred Heart.[6] And Mary MacKillop always understood God's Will as issuing from God's infinitely-loving Person. Only in this way was it possible for her to live with the Will of God.

## Living with the Way we Speak about the Will of God

Language associated with the Will of God may be a block to our feeling at home with the Will of God spirituality today. Mary MacKillop frequently used words such as 'submitting' or 'resigning' oneself to the Will of God. Julian Tenison Woods spoke about 'having no will of one's own'. It is all the language of surrender and capitulation. The idea of yielding oneself to the Will of God was originally central to the charism and mission of the Sisters of St Joseph of the Sacred Heart. But the *quasi*-military vocabulary of surrendering, with associations of 'no go' areas and laying down one's weapons, is uncongenial to modern ears. We need a new vocabulary that will enable us to live with, and be more accepting of, the Will of God.

There are some very expressive words that have a more positive and creative sense of being open to the Will of God. For example, 'supple' is a word used to describe leather, or a willow tree bending in the wind. That is a lovely image for how our wills need to be. 'Malleable' is used to describe metal being hammered into a new shape without fracturing, and without tending to return to its previous shape. As applied to our wills it suggests the adventure and even the risk involved in obeying God's Will. 'Porous' is used of rock that has no resistance to water. Someone whose will is porous has been transformed from recalcitrance into a gentle acquiescence. There are also words like 'pliable', 'mobile' and 'flexible' which describe a readiness to be changed or formed into new shapes. These words have many more possibilities for how we do God's Will than 'surrendering', 'capitulating' and 'submitting', all of which suggest the idea of giving up, which was not in Mary MacKillop's mind, nor in Evelyn Underhill's. The words 'supple', 'malleable', 'porous' and so on fit into Mary MacKillop's surprisingly creative way of understanding the Will of God as the Master Artist at work in our lives. Her main concern was how the individual human will responded to the Will of God, so as to allow God the freedom to create God's masterpiece. A person's will is analogous to the medium with which our Creator God works. God knows our limitations. We may have to be 'flexible' or 'supple' regarding some matters, or we risk hindering God's work of art, but our attitude needs to be one of co-operation or co-creation, not submission or resignation.

# Mary MacKillop's Spirituality of Living with the Will of God

The spirituality of living with the Will of God is a spirituality of experience. It has nothing visionary or mystical about it. The Will of God was the solid rock of Mary MacKillop's life.

Mary MacKillop's religious name was Mary of the Cross but it could just as truly have been Mary of the Will of God. Daniel Lyne has written about Mary MacKillop's spiritual life in the following way:

> Mary MacKillop saw an acceptance of a resignation to the Will of God as one of the foundational pivots of her spiritual life.[7]

Daniel Lyne uses the dynamic word 'pivot' to describe how Mary saw the Will of God. A pivot is a point on which something oscillates and moves. In other words, when her will was in alignment with the Will of God, the result was a vibrant, growing point in her life, not a point of capitulation. She knew that God is infinitely greater than God's Will. God is mystery and the Will of God invites us into the mystery of creative love.

Creative love is not something that is neat and tidy, and comfortable to be involved with. There is something appealing about the creative process, but usually we see the finished work of art, displayed in all its glory; we have not been present in the messy studio during its creation. We have not seen the agonising birth pangs of creation. A few years ago I visited a remarkable Rodin exhibition in Canberra. It was a revealing experience. Previously I had seen his most famous statue, *The Kiss*. I was impressed at the Canberra exhibition by the arduous work that had gone into the making of each of the finished, life-size, bronze statues. Rodin made a model first and then used scaling-up devices to get his sculptures sized-up accurately from his models. There were many castings before the deftly-delineated masterpieces emerged. There were at least five bronze studies just of a left hand in a clasping position. The creative process had been costly in terms of patience, time and effort, as well as financially, all of which is taken for granted when we go round a gallery. The mystery of God's creative love at work in our lives is the costly, infinitely painstaking lengths to which God will go to achieve God's Will for each one of us. When we realise this we long to be pliable and mobile. We cannot let our wills be hard and resistant, like obstinate knots in a piece of wood that is being transformed into a masterpiece.

For both Mary MacKillop, a religious Sister, and Evelyn Underhill, a lay retreat leader, the Will of God was neither oppressively burdensome, nor was it as set and structured as a plan. For them, God's Will was mysterious, delightfully creative, and always God's love active in our lives, like a divine dancer who is inviting us to try new steps. Evelyn Underhill speaks of our need to grow into a more and more perfect union with God's creative will. She challenged a group of priests and ministers of religion with the question:

> Do you see the great facts and splendours of religion with the eye of an artist and a lover, or with the eye of a man of business, or the eye of the man in the street?[8]

People have viewed the Will of God differently: as a plan, as 'what will be will be' – *Que sera, sera*, a catchy song but spiritually a dead end – or as the creative hand of God at work in our lives. Evelyn Underhill's challenging question is very relevant for us all. We can either look at the Passion and self-giving of Jesus to his last drop of blood, with the calculating eye of a business woman, the careless eye of a woman in the street or the creative eye of an artist. How positive or creative are we about what God is doing in our lives? Are we alert to see exciting possibilities beginning to take shape? Do we look earnestly for God's love active in our lives? For Mary MacKillop and Evelyn Underhill, God's Will was a constant invitation to be a creative artist with the materials life has provided us with.

## Living with the Rule

Mary MacKillop regarded the Rule and later the Constitution as particular expressions of God's Will for the Sisters. She writes in her circular for the Feast of the Annunciation 1873:

> Let us have no will but that of our God – and let us see this will in our Rule and in its teachings and in the wishes of our lawful Superiors.

Joyfully living with the Will of God, as it is expressed in the Rule, was to be the means of a Sister's formation or transformation, in relation to which she was to be malleable or supple, offering no resistance to the creative process. But this is easier said than done. Thinking of the days of Destinations, and being sent to some dreaded location, brings to mind a story about a little Scottish lad who used to say his prayers regularly. The family lived in Edinburgh and the time came when they were to move to Glasgow, much to the boy's dismay, for he didn't want to leave his schoolmates and his home. On the morning they were due to depart he was saying his prayers and his mother overheard him finishing with the words: 'Goodbye God! We're going to live in Glasgow!'

Living with the Will of God could involve hard assignments for Sisters: the continual interruptions of life, moving away from the known into the unknown, at times being unreasonably circumscribed and seeing no obvious plan or reason in what was happening. It was the price they paid for not living behind walls. They were to be available to go where they were sent.

Mary MacKillop lived with the Will of God in fear of impeding God's Will. She would rather do anything than be an obstacle in the way of God's Will. She wrote to Julian Tenison Woods on 2 June 1867:

> I must only trust in the mercies of God, and pray that His will be done in all things … I have begged our blessed Lord to … take me, all of us out of the world rather than suffer us to act in any other way than as he wished.

Mary MacKillop is saying that she would rather die than hinder God's Will. Elsewhere she wrote:

> So few give their wills entirely to God but may we not try to be some of the few?[9]

When she wrote 'His will be done in all things,' Mary MacKillop had the Rule very much in mind. Julian Tenison Woods had just drawn up the first Rule for the proposed Institute. Mary MacKillop saw the Rule as she saw the later Constitutions, as an expression of the Will of God for the Sisters. In response, they were to give themselves entirely to God by living according to the Rule. So giving their will entirely to God was not a vague abrogation of their will. It meant allowing God to guide their lives through the Rule. It was not a matter of following a plan but of allowing themselves to be moulded or formed by the Will of God as it was manifest in their Rule. It would be a mistake to think of the Will of God as the way in which God companions us or journeys with us. God's Will, as it was manifested in the Rule, was formative. It was to be the means of the Sisters' transformation in the process of becoming holy (whole) women.

The key to understanding Mary MacKillop's attitude to living with the Will of God in her life is to be found in the letter she wrote to Monsignor Kirby on Ascension Thursday, 1873:

> I feel a joy when things go well, for I see His will in this, and an equal joy when they seem to go wrong or against our natural desires, for there again I see His will.

It is when things go wrong that we doubt the Will of God and so in a sense we no longer live with the Will of God. But Mary saw the Will of God in everything. It did not matter whether things turned out as she wanted or not. She writes:

> (I)n comparison with it (God's Will) nothing, no sacrifice, no suffering, seemed great or even worthy of the name.

She was totally committed to doing the Will of God as it presented itself to her.

It was the completeness of her faithfulness to the claims of the Will of God that shows us her attitude as one of great love and adoration.

Mary wrote these words when she had brought the Rule to Rome for the Vatican's approval. For her to write in such an open way when there was so much at stake for her and the Institute shows a remarkable trust in God's Will. The short extract from her letter also shows that the Will of God was deeply involved in what was coming into being. It was actively at work in shaping what was to come, like a sculptor crafting a statue out of stone. From this, we realise that she saw God's Will in everything, whether it was what she wanted or not. She counted it all joy. The difficulties she encountered were never just adverse circumstances; they were the new shape of what her loving God was bringing into being, beside which her own wishes did not matter. She was open or porous, offering no resistance or hindrance to the way God chose to disclose God's Will.

Evelyn Underhill used to tell her retreatants that:

> The essence of the spiritual life was profound submission to the mysterious Will of God declared in circumstances.[10]

She speaks of the Will of God being declared 'in circumstances', by which she means everyday circumstances, the rough and tumble of their ordinary lives. This is where they would normally be aware of the Will of God. However, they may expect to experience the Will of God as closing doors – blocking or impeding their way – and sometimes it does this. This is why they need a 'profound submission' to the Will of God. By 'profound submission' she means that they have a deep desire to yield to the mysterious Will of God. It is mysterious because they do not know why things have turned out in one way rather than another. But part of their profound submission is that, although they do not understand why, they accept it is the Will of God. However, they do not resign themselves to it. She urges them to be supple, a word she uses quite frequently, so that they can be ready for whatever the loving, creative Will of God is going to bring about next, working within their circumstances, to delight them with something new, even although at times it may not feel like that.

## Living with the Story

Mary MacKillop allows us another glimpse of her view of the Will of God when she writes:

> To me the Will of God is a dear book which I am never tired of reading[11]

Everybody has a favourite story book that we never tire of reading. We enjoy the twists and turns in the plot and admire how the author leads the reader through the labyrinth to the final denouement. Mary MacKillop tells us that the Will of God is a book that is dear to her, telling the wonderful story of all that God has done and is continuing to do in her life and the development of the Institute. For example, Josephite schools around Brisbane in the 1870s had become very popular, attracting pupils away from schools run by the Sisters of Mercy, who pointed out that the Bishop would be upset if they lost the Government grant because pupil numbers were falling. Mary's response was to visit the families whose children had left the Mercy schools and persuade them to send their children back. In return, the Mercies started sending vocations to the Josephites, who were able to expand their work of teaching among the poor. Mary MacKillop could speak of 'the beautiful, wise Will of God' because she saw the Will of God operating in difficult and apparently adverse circumstances to protect and encourage the work of the Institute in surprising ways.

As she reads the story she is able to see that all the messiness of life has been transformed into a surprising pattern by the wondrous, mysteriously loving Will of God. Karl Rahner uses the word 'ambiguous' to describe how things look to us when we are in the midst of whatever life is bringing our way. More often than not, our experiences are ambiguous – messy, complex, having different aspects, some good, some bad – and we cannot properly understand the nature of what we are passing through. The Will of

God in Mary MacKillop's life was like a writer's inspiration for a story that had yet to be told, and was to transform the history of the Australian people. We each have our own story. We are bearers of stories, in which we can find God's creative will at work, mysteriously bringing into being what we could never have done for ourselves or by ourselves.

## Living with the Adorable Will of God

Just as we need new terms, such as 'supple', 'malleable', 'porous' and 'mobile', to speak about our wills and how we can respond creatively to God, so we need different language to speak about God's Will. Mary MacKillop and Evelyn Underhill can be of help. A word that they both used frequently was 'adorable'. But the adorable Will of God is not just a matter of words. 'Living with' means that you experience the adorable Will of God. Adoration comes from an experience of the unsurpassable goodness and love of God. Evelyn Underhill maintains that the right attitude to God is supported by the prayer of pure adoration. No matter how much time we have for private prayer, half of it should be spent in such adoration.

In her circular for St Joseph's Day 1893, Mary MacKillop speaks several times of 'the adorable Will of God'. 'Adorable' is not a word most people would choose to describe the Will of God. 'Adorable' is the passionate language that a lover uses of his beloved. For Mary MacKillop, the Will of God was beloved and she rejoiced to be living with it. No matter how hard it was for her to do what God's Will was asking of her – and she tells us she found it hard – it was still the loved will of a loving and beloved God. What we adore overwhelms us and banishes all thought of self and self-will. Mary MacKillop knew that by adoring the Will of God, being creatively attentive to God's mysterious will, hidden in the cloud of all that was happening to her, she would be empowered to collaborate with God's Will in whatever new circumstances her loving God was bringing into being.

Evelyn Underhill talks of the 'adoring, self-oblivious vision'[12] that is given from beyond ourselves as a gift from God. Adoration is also a theme that runs through her retreat addresses. She writes:

> In … a prayer of adoring attentiveness, we open our doors wide to receive his (God's) ever-present Spirit … The remedy for that sense of impotence, that desperate, spiritual exhaustion which religious workers too often know, is, I am sure, an inner life governed … by adoring prayer.[13]

When we listen in prayer with wholehearted attentiveness to hear God's voice, we are adoring God. We are holding nothing back when we open our hearts to receive God's Spirit. If we are suffering from spiritual exhaustion and weariness, the answer is to lift our spirits in adoration away from ourselves and self-pity to God. We lift our hearts up to God in adoring prayer. Evelyn Underhill speaks of 'a steady approximation to more and more perfect union with his (God's) creative will'.[14] This means that we go more and more at God's pace, not our own, because we are living with the adorable Will of God. In her retreat talks, *The Light of Christ*, Evelyn Underhill urges her retreatants to respond to life where it finds them and to wait, to grow and change, not according to their preconceived notions of pace, but according to the will and pace of God. This is indeed to live with and to experience the adorable Will of God.

Both Mary MacKillop and Evelyn Underhill suffered from chronic ill-health, yet they lived full and busy lives. Through their acceptance of the overruling will and pace of God, they were instruments or channels for God's creative will to reach others.

Living with the Will of God was a challenging and creative experience for both of these remarkable women. There was nothing burdensome about it. It was particularly costly for Mary MacKillop, who had to live through opposition, animosity and injustice. She was enabled to do so always with forgiveness, because her will was malleable and porous to whatever circumstances God allowed to come in her way. She responded creatively with love because she lived with the Will of God.

# 4

# *Revisiting the Virtue of*
# *Humility with Mary MacKillop*

## The Need to Revisit Humility

If people today were asked what they thought the most important
virtue was, they would probably select love, or faith, patience or
courage. Humility would not rate highly, although it might be
regarded as an optional extra for those who wanted to excel in
virtue and piety. It was a different matter for Mary MacKillop, for
whom humility was supremely important.

In this present age of self-expression and competitiveness, with
its mind-set of individualism, focusing on the rights and entitle-
ments of the individual, humility has become a neglected and
unpopular virtue. Indeed, it is not clear how, in a society of noisy
litigation, there can be a place for humility. However, today's
society is not solely to blame. Part of the difficulty is that humility
has a history of misrepresentation. It is a fragile virtue, easily
distorted and misunderstood. If we were to ask what humility
means today, it would be connected in the minds of many with
having a poor opinion of oneself and low self-esteem. If that were
indeed the true meaning of humility, it would hardly be worth
revisiting. As we shall see, Mary MacKillop did not necessarily
connect humility with self-abasement. Recently, several notable
spiritual writers, including Joan Chittister[1] and Esther de Waal,[2]
have written to the effect that the true meaning of humility has
been lost and needs to be reclaimed. Mary MacKillop would
certainly agree.

## The Importance of Humility to Mary MacKillop

It would generally be known that Mary MacKillop frequently
wrote about the Will of God, but not so well known that, over

thirty years, she devoted a considerable amount of attention to the virtue of humility. In a letter to Father Julian Tenison Woods,[3] written from Brisbane in 1870, she presented what could be described as a mini-treatise on the subject. Over twenty years later (1893), her circular to the Sisters for the feast day of the Institute's patron, St Joseph,[4] highlighted humility. In *The Book of Instructions*,[5] written in 1907, two years before she died, a substantial section is concerned with humility. Her view that humility was vitally important for the spiritual wellbeing of the Sisters had not changed for over almost forty years. It could be argued that humility used to be the hallmark of Josephite formation. It is not at all obvious that humility is central to formation today.

I shall address two questions in this short chapter, the remainder of which is divided into two parts. The first part deals with the question: Why did Mary MacKillop set such store by humility? The second part deals with the question: How can she help us to reclaim humility as an inspiring virtue for our lives today?

## Mary MacKillop's Views on Humility

In her letter to Father Woods (1870), she distinguished between what she calls 'true' and 'false' humility, showing that she was well aware that some so-called humble behaviour was not an expression of genuine humility. As Father Paul Gardiner explains, 'What she is saying is like saying "there are two kinds of gold, fools' gold and real gold".'[6] Mary MacKillop had a clear understanding of what might easily be mistaken for humility, but which on her reckoning was counterfeit. She writes:

> (False humility) ... seems to covet in its possessor every kind of opprobrium and censure from its fellow creatures, without the slightest regard to what it may cost many good souls, to entertain doubtful thoughts of another whom they would fain esteem, but whose actions and expressions they cannot understand.[7]

Her way of speaking does not resonate with today's idiomatic language, but it is not hard to understand what she is saying, if we consider our own experience. We have probably all come across people who tiresomely seem to enjoy belittling their achievements, in the name of humility. What they are actually doing, however, is drawing attention to them. Sometimes a person may receive an uncharitable or unjust slur from another, without making any attempt to correct the false impression because she believes it will keep her humble. It is more likely to lead to a loss of self-esteem, as well as perplexing others who do not know what to think. This so-called humility is 'selfish ... cold ... studied' (Mary's terms) because it is concerned with personal ambitions of reaching unrealistic pinnacles of virtue. Studying to present oneself as humble is inverted pride and is paradoxically self-defeating. What results is a grotesque parody. The prime example of this in literature is the character of Uriah Heap, in Dickens' novel *David Copperfield*, who believed that by describing himself as 'the 'umblest person going', and behaving accordingly, he would ingratiate himself with others. Mary MacKillop has rightly identified an attitude that is contrary to real humility because it masks pride and an inflated sense of self, and consequently diminishes a proper sense of self and self-worth.

On the other hand, according to Mary MacKillop, genuine humility is grounded on truth, and a truly humble person acknowledges her own self-worth rather than allowing others to labour under misconceptions about her. She writes:

> True humility ... is accompanied by a sweet and thoughtful charity ... It troubles not itself about either the esteem or censure of creatures.[8]

True humility is inspired by charity and thoughtfulness for others. It is not concerned with self or one's failings or what others think about one. It is the antidote to both self-importance and loss of self-esteem. She acknowledged that there are different ways in which true humility might be expressed, but for the Sisters all behaviour that drew attention to itself was to be avoided.[9] However, humility is commonly associated with not taking any credit and taking the lowest position. Occasionally Mary MacKillop advised the Sisters to take the lowest position.[10] But in her letter to Father Woods, she was concerned with true humility as an inner disposition that was free from any illusions about self-importance, grounded in reality and an acceptance of the truth about oneself and others. For Mary MacKillop, humility brought freedom of mind, by which she did not mean a *laissez-faire* attitude of thinking and doing as you please, but rather the ability to see things as they really are and to be grounded in truth, which is consistent with the derivation of humility from the Latin *humus*, meaning ground or soil. It is the ground of a person's being, to adapt a phrase used by Tillich.[11] She regards humility as the selfless, creative environment of charity, from which our true humanity grows. Humility or freedom from self-distortion is the fertile soil that ensures other virtues will take root and grow, because they are liberated from a self-centred preoccupation with 'being virtuous', and so leave a person free to love and serve God and others wholeheartedly. Humility is far from being an optional extra, in Mary MacKillop's view, but is the necessary foundation for a well-grounded spiritual life.

## How Can Mary MacKillop Help Us to Reclaim Humility as a Focus for Our Lives Today?

Mary's distinction between true and false humility is of major importance in helping us to unravel confusions about humility in our thinking today. A present day confusion that is similar to the confusion between true and false humility is between humility and humiliation, both of which are derived from the Latin *humus*. It is not difficult to see how the confusion has arisen. To humiliate means to bring another down. For example, the victorious side in battle humiliates the opposing side by defeating them. Similarly, an individual humiliates another by belittling or debasing him or her and metaphorically crushing the other to the ground. Unfortunately, there has been a mistaken tendency to think that one way of becoming humble is to suffer humiliation. A person may even relish humiliation, believing self-abasement would be spiritually beneficial, but what results is low self-esteem and a poor self-image, which is not the true meaning of humility and is not, as we have seen, what Mary MacKillop understood by humility. Humiliation is destructive behaviour and is likely to be personally damaging to the one being humiliated, failing to encourage a properly grounded estimate of self.

Humility in its true sense, however, is already coming back into vogue. Joan Chittister, in her recent study of St Benedict's theory of humility writes, 'Humility is the virtue of liberation from self that makes us available to the wisdom of others.'[12] And Esther de Waal also maintains that humility is 'having a proper sense of self. It means knowing and accepting my limitations, and not denying them.'[13] Both writers recognise that humility is connected with the ability to have a well-grounded assessment of oneself in relation to others. This, I believe, is how Mary MacKillop understood true humility, which is based on charity that diverts attention away from the self to love of others and God, as opposed to false humility, which centres on self in isolation from others and ensures loss of perspective.

## Josephite Humility – an Inspirational Virtue for Today

The virtue of humility has a long history of significance for the Congregation of the Sisters of St Joseph. It was as central to Mary MacKillop's spirituality, as it is to Ignatian spirituality,[14] with which she was familiar.[15] The main reason for humility's importance to Mary MacKillop was the Founders' choice of St Joseph as Patron of the new Institute in 1867.[16] It is clear that Mary MacKillop wanted the Sisters to regard St Joseph as their model, particularly in relation to his humility. In her circular to the Sisters for 19 March 1893, she wrote:

> This humility ... is something wonderfully beautiful in itself ... My Sisters, his was a quiet humility ... a humility of heart, not of words ... a silent not a noisy humility.[17]

Why did Mary MacKillop regard St Joseph's humility as inspirational for the Sisters? What did she hope it would inspire the Sisters to do or be in their Religious life? In the first place, St Joseph was the model of true humility that leads to an inner freedom of heart. Secondly, humility was the key to living life in a spirit of poverty. And, finally, humility was the means of preserving unity. What can we learn from her approach to inspire us to live well as Christians in today's society?

## Humility and Heart Freedom

The quality of St Joseph's humility that specially attracted Mary MacKillop was its quiet hiddenness. There was nothing on show and it did not parade itself. St Joseph was the prime example of true humility. Elsewhere, she writes: 'St Joseph, our father, was humble and hidden.'[18] St Joseph had an in-depth humility that was an inner disposition of the heart or will. The humility Mary MacKillop so much admired was an ingrained tendency to look beyond self to the good of others, as Joseph looked beyond the opinions of others to his care of Mary and Jesus. It was St Joseph's selflessness that Mary MacKillop especially wished her Sisters to emulate, because it enabled a person to be authentic. This is further explained in the same circular, when she speaks of St Joseph being aware of 'his own nothingness'.[19] She did not mean by that that St Joseph regarded himself as having no value or significance. What she meant is brought out in the following verse:

> A man that looks on glass
> On it may stay his eye;
> Or if he pleaseth, through it pass
> And then the heavens espy.
> (George Herbert)

When we look through a window we are not aware of the glass unless there is a mark or stain on it. There is a sense in which the glass is nothing, or hidden, and serves only to show the view beyond. Like a transparent window pane, the Sisters' lives were to be selfless or free from self in order to be the clear medium through which people may glimpse eternity and divine love. To be humble, like St Joseph, a Sister must, through her selflessness, display the love of God in her actions and behaviour. No self-glory was to discolour the glass of her life and block the transparency. Selfish ambition would not have any place in a life that flowed from a liberated self, free enough to live solely for love of God and the good of others.

This Christ-like humility is a radical forgetfulness of self that goes beyond being a social virtue of unselfishness and consideration for others. It is the wellspring of the heart that creatively embraces the Will of God as one's destiny. This charitable humility is as vital today as it was in Mary MacKillop's day. It is not for the faint-hearted but neither is it exclusively for religious. It expands the understanding of what is humanly possible. It is a humility that takes risks and constantly adventures beyond the known. It is the stuff that saints are made of, and is the doorway through which the divine can access suffering and affliction in the world. Josephites today are called to be pioneers in selflessness. People will always need to see that it is possible to live beyond the parameters of self-interest and be inspired to try themselves, for by doing so they are free to engage with reality.

## Humility and Poverty

Mary MacKillop saw an important connection between humility and poverty. Writing about the spirit of St Joseph that was to inspire the Sisters, she says:

> The spirit of the Sisters of St Joseph is a spirit of poverty … Poverty and humility go hand in hand. If our poverty is not humble poverty it will not last … we must never consider ourselves, but only our work and be ready to do it wherever it is to be done.[20]

In society today, which is preoccupied with the standard of living, poverty, like humility, is regarded as something to be avoided. However, by poverty Mary MacKillop did not just mean financial poverty but rather being poor in spirit which meant the acceptance of complete dependence upon, and trust in, God. This poverty of spirit enabled them to have a grasp of reality.

She also connected humble poverty with the work of the Institute, which had been founded to be an option for the poor. As she herself declared, 'St Joseph's schools are humble, intended only for the humble poor'.[21] In her view, it was important that their poverty was humble because, unless it was, it would not last. There were two points about humble poverty that she wanted the Sisters to grasp. Firstly, the Sisters were to be followers of the Jesus of humility, who himself thought nothing of becoming a servant and washing his disciples' feet. He responded to a real need with an actual loving act of humility, that went far beyond the habits and customs of the time and could well have incurred censure from his critics, had they been present. Secondly, the Sisters' humble service of the poor called them to be one with the poor and to live alongside the poor. If they ceased to accept the reality of their own poverty and the needs of the poor they were to serve, Mary MacKillop feared the work would come to an end, for they would no longer be depending upon God but on themselves, nor would they be putting the needs of the poor first but, rather, government educational policy and aid. They were to be followers of Jesus, 'who went to the poor like steel to a magnet (and) was poor himself'.[22]

Mary MacKillop's connection between humility and poverty prompts us to reconsider our attitude to the poor today. The many kinds of poverty in the world are almost beyond comprehension. In the wake of disasters, natural and man-made, people respond with generous financial aid out of their own affluence, but the poor and destitute are a remote idea for many, or, more concretely, pictures on the TV news. But images of the poor and destitute do not help us to be connected with real poverty. Helen Prejean speaks about the change in her life when she heard a speaker at a meeting on justice quote the text: 'I bring good news for the poor' (Luke 4:18), adding that the good news was that they would no longer be poor. Helen recognised a call to her to do something more than pray for the poor. She was being challenged to be with them in their poverty. This conviction eventually led her to 'walk' with those on Death Row. A few individuals may be inspired to go and be with those suffering in areas affected by earthquakes and tsunamis, but in general people continue to strive for success, power and status in a society where such things have priority. The poor remain images on our TV screens and continue to be idealised and kept at a safe distance.

Jean Vanier is today's prophet of humility and service of the poor. He points out that, when Jesus called the disciples to take the lowest place, he was not just urging them to fight against pride and the need to be important. He was inviting them to sit with the poor, to become poor themselves, for there they would encounter the presence of God:

> Jesus tells us that by taking the lowest place we will meet the poor, the weak, the crippled, the blind and the outcast, who are all signs of the presence of God. As we become their friends, we become friends of God.[23]

God still calls individuals today to stop climbing the ladder of promotion and striving for success, but to mix with the poor, the oppressed, refugees and asylum seekers, and people with AIDS in Africa, for there they will surely discover the presence of God. Revisiting Mary MacKillop's understanding of humility can inspire us today to test just how realistic our attitude is to the poor in our midst, and how prepared we are to be inspired by the Josephite charism, constantly and selflessly to serve and be with those who have been left at the margins of society.

## Unity – the Fruit of Humility

Frequently in her writings, Mary MacKillop connected humility with unity. In a letter written to the Sisters on 30 September 1873, she urged them: 'Be faithful to your Rule, remain firmly united, diffident in yourselves.'[24] 'Diffident' is a word that is not much in use today. What Mary MacKillop meant by the phrase, 'diffident in yourselves,' was not to be overconfident but be humble, allow for the possibility that you could be wrong. A Sister did not have the right to criticise another and find fault, because to do so was to put herself on a pedestal, thereby introducing division. There is a very plausible and practical connection between not thinking too highly of oneself and unity, in the sense that self-importance refuses to allow others to have their rightful place, which in turn causes resentment and disunity.

In her Circular to the Sisters for September 4th 1906, she wrote:

> Sisters of St Joseph should never love their own opinions ... Let us be ready to give way. We are never sure that we are right; and even when we are nearly sure let us not contend. When we have given our opinion humbly and quietly, let us sacrifice the rest for love of God.[25]

She knew very well how easily unity could be damaged in Josephite communities, through gossip, bickering, murmuring, criticism and fault finding.[26] Those who engaged in these 'faults of the tongue' had an inflated sense of their own importance. They lacked humility and they were the cause of disunity. Over and over in her writings, Mary MacKillop urged the Sisters to maintain their unity, often asking them to be forgiving towards one another.

Of course, she is not saying that the Sisters are not to have opinions. What she is saying is that they are not to be opinionated, that is, so attached to their own opinions and self-importance that they cannot listen to the opinions of others. Humility teaches us wisdom to know that we can never be absolutely certain that we are right. Others have a right to their points of view. Sisters of St Joseph are to be ready to give way, not out of weakness, but for the love of God and the sake of unity. For many reasons, disunity is to be avoided. If there is no unity: firstly, the Sisters cannot live together in charity; secondly, their witness as an Institute is weakened; thirdly, they will be ineffective in their ministry; and fourthly, they will not be prepared to listen to others. However, when there is an attitude of humility that willingly allows others to express their opinions, the voice of God may be more easily discerned and disunity avoided.

Mary MacKillop gave practical advice on the importance of humility in relation to unity. Her advice to the Sisters to be humble and open enough to listen to others and be prepared to give way, is something we need to hear today and be able to apply at all levels of society, from the personal level of broken relationships to a national level of finding ways to heal divisions within society between ethnic groups, those within the system and those who are excluded, refugees and asylum seekers; between weak and strong, rich and poor. There is a brokenness in today's society that cannot be properly addressed as long as self-importance and a competitive spirit are considered acceptable. We need to reconsider the virtue of humility as the antidote to self-importance and its consequence of disunity.

In today's pluralist society in particular, there is an urgent need to listen to the 'other', if there is to be peace between those of different religious persuasions. Tolerance is needed, and also respect for those who are different from ourselves, but humility is even more urgently needed, especially in relation to inter-religious dialogue, where there is the mutual need to learn from one another. Joan Chittister writes: 'Humility lies in learning to listen to the words, directions and insights of those around us. They are the voice of God calling to us here and now.'[27]

But we will not hear God's voice in the 'other' unless we are inspired humbly to accept ourselves, others and the reality of life as it is. Huston Smith writes perceptively about humility: 'Humility is not self-abasement. It is the capacity to regard oneself in the company of others as one but not more than one.'[28]

This modern definition of humility is in keeping with Mary MacKillop's aspirations for the Sisters regarding St Joseph's quiet humility, that does not seek limelight but is the answer to our self-importance which is so inimical to inner peace and under-mining of relationships. In a society where relationships founder and are put at risk, it is surely worth revisiting a virtue that has been described as 'the mortar of relationships',[29] which can have a healing effect in people's lives.

Joan Chittister writes: 'The twenty-first century has plenty to relearn about humility.'[30] Humility was of great importance to Mary MacKillop, who spoke about it as 'God's school'.[31] The first thing we need to relearn is the true meaning of humility. Mary MacKillop can help us to do this by her distinction between true and false humility. St Joseph was the model of humility, to whose selfless spirit of humble poverty she urged the Sisters to turn for inspiration. Humility is the great teacher of reality. It teaches us to be real about ourselves and others and also frees us from illusions about always being right. Humility teaches us about the reality of our own poverty and enables us to be in touch with the poor. Finally, humility is the ground from which unity within communities and society will be achieved, because it fosters self-respect and respect for the other.

Mary's perceptive remarks about humility apply today and can inspire and challenge us radically to question the degree to which self-importance and competitiveness are admired in today's society. Just as she valiantly confronted disunity in her day, so Mary MacKillop can be an inspiration to us to ground our lives on the truth of who we are, and an acceptance of others who are different, as the presence of God in our lives – those whom we neglect at our peril.

# 5

## The Vow of Poverty – Mary MacKillop and Julian Tenison Woods

*What Religious life needs now, if vows are to be worth anything at all, is a fresh and challenging call to a new understanding of poverty, one that engages this entire generation of religious in the process of living poverty for the sake of the poor.*

Joan Chittister OSB

If there had been no poverty in Australia in the nineteenth century, there would not have been the same need for the Sisters of Saint Joseph of the Sacred Heart. Poverty and the Sisters went hand-in-hand. Had there been no cry of the poor for them to respond to, they would each have continued on their paths in very different lives. But the cry they heard was the cry of children in desperate need of education and of families unable to care for them because they were in such dire straits themselves. Poverty was the hard ground in which they planted a seed of hope by becoming poor themselves.

They knew they were called to work and to love amid poverty. All who joined this Institute were to be prepared to live among and like the poor whom they were serving.[1] To be poor and to be founded on poverty was the way the Sisters came into being. There was no other way to reach the children with the education they needed.

Mary MacKillop and Julian Tenison Woods had strong views about poverty. Julian was an idealist and he wanted the Institute he had founded to be 'pure'. He believed he could achieve this by poverty: having no property, money or possessions. Mary's family had known poverty. All her life they were either in debt or borrowing money or a place to live from relatives. Poverty was no stranger to her. They were perpetually short of money. When it came to founding an institute and founding it on poverty, it was nothing new to her.

The mention of poverty today brings to mind destitution, begging, doing without, going hungry, not having enough money, being in want, and so on – all very negative associations. Poverty is hard to come to terms with, especially in Religious life, because we no longer live in poverty even though we have taken a vow of poverty. We live without the insecurities that many people have today. We need to clarify what we mean when we talk about poverty. We need to be prophets of poverty, standing firm on the call to give and give still more to the poor. We vow to live a life that is exemplified by the poor Christ and to centre our hearts on Him. By doing this we undertake to be committed to the poor and to live a simple lifestyle of sharing. Religious need to be whole-hearted stewards of their resources. There is very little hardship today in the life we have chosen. I believe that Mary MacKillop's understanding of poverty can bring us face to face with the challenge of the vow of poverty we have taken.

When Mary MacKillop took a vow of poverty, she knew that she was choosing to live with the risk of being without adequate money or food for the rest of her life. She knew she would have to beg for herself, her Sisters and the children in her care. Mary had a firm trust in the providence of God, so she knew they would not starve, and she had a vision of the Sisters, poor themselves, reaching out to poor children. It was this vision that lifted them above their own discomforts to the joy of bringing little children love and a knowledge of a loving God. Today, when Sisters take a vow of poverty they know that they are not going to be radically short of money and certainly not deprived of adequate food, although they may not be able to afford every little luxury they might fancy. There is a difference between how the vow of poverty was lived in the time of Mary MacKillop and how the vow is lived today. In their mission of educating poor children, the Sisters' vow of poverty would have enabled them to identify with poor families. The Sisters had to learn to live without what they were accustomed to think of as necessary.

In Australia, in the nineteenth century, when girls joined the Institute they very often had little or no money. No dowry was asked for, nor was it expected. It was an altogether different culture, of fortune seekers, gold rushes and gold diggers. There were many impoverished people in the society of the time: those who did not strike it lucky. For Mary MacKillop, all were equal and, whether rich or poor, deserved to be treated equally. There was also spiritual poverty, which was as important to the Sisters as material poverty. It was spiritual poverty that Mary MacKillop was keen that they understood and lived.

At the beginning of the Institute, Mary and Julian were asking of the Sisters what to us would be extreme poverty. Neither the Institute nor individual Sisters were to own property. To begin with, their grounding in poverty was a bond between them. Although Julian had never lived in poverty, as Mary had, they shared the same ideas for the Institute: that it was to be, as it were, an extension of the world of the poor, with the same bare necessities and few comforts.

When Mary MacKillop spoke of being poor she very often meant being spiritually poor, which had nothing to do with needing money but rather being completely dependent upon God. They needed to be poor in order to find the way to God. To have plenty was not going to help them to find God. Poverty was not an obstacle but an opening of the way for them, as it is for us. We lead a simple lifestyle in order to be able to help the poor in whatever way they need help, not as social workers but as people committed to bringing the love of God to the marginalised.

I am going to start by looking at the meaning of 'poverty' and 'poor'. They are both well used terms with a variety of meanings that have changed little since the nineteenth century. The Bible has many references to 'poor' but very few to 'poverty'. Jesus does not mention poverty at all. The reason he doesn't is that he came as a poor man among the poor to serve them and set them free to belong to the Kingdom of God, not to confront society. The Vow of Poverty is essentially to serve the poor. In order to understand why poverty was of such key importance for Julian and Mary, we need to grasp the connection in their thinking between poverty and property. Whether rightly or wrongly, no ownership was the key to poverty for them. Owning nothing meant that there was nothing for anyone to be possessive about. As newly founded, the identity of the Institute was fragile. What was essential to it and what could be modified was of great moment to Julian Tenison Woods, because Rome had sanctioned changes to his rules on ownership.[2] Finally, as we look at the spirituality of poverty and the associated concepts of dependence on God and detachment, we shall find that the true meaning of poverty for Religious life in today's world is simplicity of life style, which is more difficult to achieve than we might think.

## The Meaning of 'Poverty' and 'Poor'

Some clarification is needed of the terms 'poverty' and 'poor' before we can embark on the importance of poverty to Mary MacKillop and Julian Tenison Woods. Poverty goes right to the roots of the Congregation of the Sisters of St Joseph of the Sacred Heart.

Poverty is the social condition of being without adequate money, food or shelter. It also has connotations of exploitation, deprivation and marginalisation. It is an involuntary state. People fall into the 'poverty trap', not of their own will but because of circumstances they often cannot help, and they find it very hard to get out of the trap once they've fallen into it.

Poverty is an umbrella term. There are other kinds of poverty that come under the umbrella of poverty. As well as involuntary poverty there is also voluntary poverty, when people choose to live frugally of their own free will, and to give their money to charity or to some good cause. Religious life has a core commitment to voluntary poverty. Religious choose to be without personal financial remuneration, salaries or stipends, because by doing without their pay they are testifying to the spiritual bond (charism) uniting them. They also choose to do so because it is a way of being closer to God. Material possessions cannot be allowed to come between a Sister (or a lay person) and God. Poverty was the basic evangelical counsel for Congregations such as the Josephites and Franciscans.[3] But every Christian is called to follow Jesus and to live in solidarity with the poor and the marginalised.

As well as involuntary and voluntary poverty, there is another kind of poverty that Mary MacKillop spoke of in the early days of the Institute, namely primitive poverty. I have never come across primitive poverty anywhere else. I do not know whether it was her own name for it or whether it would have been more generally known. By primitive poverty, she meant basic poverty, in the sense that there was absolutely no ownership, with no exceptions. Thus there was no ownership of property by the Institute and there was to be no ownership for the Sisters. They were to regard everything as lent to them, including clothes, books and furnishings. Primitive poverty is essentially concerned with total no ownership. One owns nothing. Primitive poverty is very near to spiritual poverty. The Sisters own nothing so as to learn to be completely dependent on God. It was dependence on God that enabled Mary MacKillop to live with poverty without being weighed down by it.

The term 'poor' is closely connected with poverty. Whereas poverty is a social condition, being poor tends to be a condition of the individual. To be poor is to be lacking money or other means of subsistence. We do sometimes speak of the poor collectively – when we are speaking of a social class, for example. More importantly for Religious life, there is also the condition of being spiritually poor. Someone who is poor in spirit knows she is completely dependent upon God. We can also talk about being poor in spirit, as being detached, and free from attachments, so that one can always put God first and give to God an undivided heart.

There were four senses of poverty for Mary MacKillop – *involuntary poverty, voluntary poverty, primitive poverty* and *spiritual poverty* – and there were two senses of poor – *poor in material goods,* and poor in the sense of *poor in spirit,* being dependent on God –

and lastly, poor in the sense of being detached from material possessions, which is another way of being *spiritually poor*. We need to be clear which sense Mary and Julian are talking about and what it is about poverty that was so important for them in the beginning.

## Poverty and property

The concept of poverty takes us back to the very beginning of the foundation of the Institute. Mary MacKillop wrote prior to 1875 (the first General Chapter) about 'the primitive poverty in which the Sisterhood was founded'.[4] It was primitive poverty she believed they should aim at. The Sisters did not want 'any pandering to the spirit of the world'.[5] What exactly did she mean by primitive poverty? Not all poverty is primitive. Primitive poverty is a condition of no-ownership of property, material possessions, and money. Non-primitive poverty, on the other hand, allows for some ownership.

When Mary returned from Rome in 1874 with the revised Rule, she knew she had exchanged the primitive poverty of the original Rule for non-primitive poverty, for Rome had decreed that the Institute was to own property – at least one Central House in each diocese, for the Sisters' security and well being. When she wrote to the Sisters about the changes, she said that she hoped they would be allowed to have primitive poverty again:

> I am sorry that we are allowed to possess property, and until that is finally decided, will pray that if it be God's Will, that it may yet be altered for us.[6]

She knew no ownership was what they needed in order to be free of responsibility for property that would have taken them away from their mission to bring Catholic education to children in remote parts of the bush. That, however, never happened. Rome did not change its mind. The Sisters were to be responsible for money and property. This was particularly difficult for Mary. She never wanted to possess money and, when she had it, she never had it for long.

At the founding of the Institute, it was Julian Tenison Woods who was adamant that the Sisters were not to own property. However, Mary was fully in agreement with him. As well as no ownership, the Sisters were to have only what poor people could afford. They were to live and work as poor people, go hungry or sleep on the floor, if necessary. The Sisters did not mind sleeping in dormitories, because for each to have her own room would suggest ownership and marginal independence. No other Order in Australia lived and worked alongside the people as the Josephites did.

What was the reason for the emphasis placed on primitive poverty by Julian and Mary? Firstly, if the Sisters were tied down by property they would not be able to be a mobile task force, free to come and go as and where they were needed, which was the object of their Institute. They were to be available for the people. Secondly, Julian believed that if they owned anything this would be detrimental to their dependence upon God. It would mark the beginning of their search for aid from sources other than God, such as the government. He wrote in the Rules:

> God will have his work subsist without the aid of men and it is to Him alone the Sisters must look for aid.[7]

Mary speaks of leaning so completely 'upon Providence as never to have any property of our own'. Julian wrote the following in a letter to Mary, on 23 August 1870, which shows just how committed he was to poverty:

> ... the object of our Institute is to go and teach poor schools without any aid except alms and the help that the children can afford. This is what the Sisters dedicate themselves to in honour of the Sacred Heart ... Rather than change this feature, which would be a change in the whole spirit of the Institute, they must give up the mission.[8]

Julian never altered his position on this. He is quite explicit that he would rather see the Institute dissolved than the spirit lost. 'It would be like removing the altar from a church,' he said. The altar is both the symbol of sacrifice and the table of the Lord. If the altar were removed it would be robbing the church of its purpose. As the bread and the wine are brought forward for the Eucharist, so are the offerings for the poor and the needy. As St Justin says:

> What is gathered is given to him who presides to assist orphans and widows ... all who are in need.[9]

Julian is pointing out that without the altar they would have no sense of the poor in the Mass. There would be no place for them. With no altar, the Sisters would have nowhere to make a complete offering of themselves except upon the altar of their own heart. The Church would be nothing more than an empty shell with no altar. Its purpose of serving the poor would be totally ignored, as if they did not exist, and the mission of the Institute would be lost. Julian could never allow this to happen.

What Julian was in effect saying was that an incompatibility exists between poverty and property, such that if one has property one cannot have poverty and vice versa; but there is no incompatibility. One can own property and yet be poor. It depends how the property is used, for one's selfish pleasure or to share with someone who needs a home. Rome certainly did not see any incompatibility between them and, in the end, neither did Mary. She came round to Rome's way of thinking and she saw the good sense in owning at least a Mother House. Sadly, it was the beginning of an estrangement between Mary and Julian. Julian wrote to Mary:

> It has been almost a deathblow to me to see the poverty and simplicity of the Institute of St Joseph destroyed and that without my being able to say a word in its defence.[10]

Julian did not understand how hard it had been for Mary to accept the ownership of property. All that Julian could say was that he did not see anything that would have compelled her to adopt Rome's ruling regarding property. As far as he was concerned the Rules had been completely changed and poverty and simplicity had been destroyed. He wrote to Mary:

> Am I wrong in thinking that I am sent away from the Sisters or that you mistrust my spirit or that the poverty and the simplicity of the institute are destroyed?[11]

The change in poverty deeply affected Julian. He believed that Mary was wrong ('misguided' and 'mistaken' were the words he used). The trust between them had been lost. Mary's only comfort was that she had prayed throughout that God's Will would be done.

It was a pity they gave so much attention to the issue of no ownership in the beginning because that really has very little to do with poverty. Poverty is what one does with what one owns. As Joan Chittister says:

> Using what we have for ourselves alone is the real sin against religious poverty.

## Poverty and the Identity of the Institute

The Sisters of St Joseph of the Sacred Heart had been founded on poverty. They were, in a very real sense, themselves children of poverty. Their identity as an Institute emerged from the nature of the poverty they lived. One might say that it was a radical form of poverty. It was the identification of the Sisters with the poor, except that it could never be complete identification because the Sisters' poverty was voluntary and the poverty of the poor was involuntary. The Sisters had taken a vow of poverty. The poor had no such luxury. It was the idealism of Julian that wanted to make their poverty as real as it could be in order that they might come as near as possible to involuntary poverty, and to understanding what it meant to have nothing, not from choice, but from necessity.

The emphasis on primitive poverty (owning nothing) was connected with the identity of the Institute. Julian wrote, in *The Spirit of the Institute* (1870), that:

It (the Institute) undertakes to teach poor schools without any aid except alms and what the children themselves can afford. To alter this particular would alter the whole character of the Order.[12]

Very few people, if any, he goes on to say, can understand the motive for refusing any extra financial support. What they did not realise was that this dependence on what the children could give, and alms in honour of the Sacred Heart, was the identity of the Institute. It was not just a feature of the Institute that could be changed, according to experience and advice of others. Their critics could not sympathise with the Sisters because they were unable to see that this characteristic could not be changed without destroying its identity.

Mary spoke of poverty as being the Sisters' 'mark of distinction'. To be a mark of distinction was to be the means of identification that would establish their identity. She writes, in *Adaptation of the Rules* (1867):

They are the children of poverty since the desire of working for the poor was the first thought inspired by the Holy Ghost that gave birth to the Institute.[13]

Working for the poor was the *raison d'etre* of the Institute. There were no other orders in Australia at the time that were so against ownership. Furthermore, the Josephites did away with the distinction between Choir and Lay Sisters that gave rise to inequalities, which were, in some cases, associated with wealth. So Mary could write:

Poverty is the ornament of the Institute, and should be worn by them (the Sisters) as the brightest gem which they can wear as the badge of their Divine Spouse.[14]

Mary had written this in praise of poverty. An ornament that someone wears can be very striking in its beauty. It is what people will notice. Indeed, poverty is 'the brightest gem' they can wear. It is precious, and to be worn with a certain pride because Christ himself lived in poverty and the Sisters were to follow him and the disciples.

The identity of a thing cannot be tampered with. To say that poverty is the identity of the Institute is like saying my fingerprints are my identity. This would explain why Julian was so adamant that if property and ownership became acceptable to the Institute it would necessarily herald its demise. It would no longer be the Institute he founded.

## Debt and Poverty[15]

Once Central Government had decreed that the Sisters were to own property, Mary ceased to talk about whether they should own property or not. Rome had spoken on the matter. Owning property when the Sisters had no money led them into a minefield of difficulties. They had to live with debts and the accumulating interest on borrowed money. They were unable to pay their way, especially in South Australia. It was a poor colony. Friends, like the Barr Smiths, often came to the Sisters' rescue. This became a new aspect of being poor. They owned property but could not pay for it. Living with no money was one thing but living with the burden of debt was something else. Rome appeared to be indifferent to their plight, and seemed not to realise that they were seriously short of money, and so was the diocese where they lived. It was very painful poverty they had to endure. The Sisters were not finally out of debt until Sister Elizabeth Murphy's time, when the Congregational Leadership Team was able to build up Reserve Funds. It was not only property that used up what little funds they had. It was fares, as they travelled from place to place as a mobile task force. It all cost money. From time to time they had to travel by sea, as they went from colony to colony, and also to New Zealand. They had to beg for their fares, when the priest did not give them money. They were constantly aware that they were poor and that they had to struggle. But they knew they were called to be poor. They had taken a vow of poverty and, in a sense, they rejoiced in their dependence on God.

## Spirituality of Poverty

We are so used today of thinking of the poor as the deprived and exploited, and of poverty as shortage of money or food, and associated bad health, that we tend to overlook the extended sense of 'poor' in which it means a 'virtue', a desirable moral quality, poor in spirit or heart. Jesus spoke of 'the poor in spirit', by which he meant the humble-minded. Mary speaks of the 'perfection of poverty', which she explains as consisting 'more in true poverty of heart than in actual privation'. It was always the motives of the heart that Mary MacKillop was concerned with. To be poor in heart is to be self-forgetful, because one is focusing on others. Diarmuid O'Murchu says, of the poor in spirit, that they are:

> Those people who are open to receive from the generous abundance of God because they know God to be radically near, immersed in the ordinariness of daily event and encounter.[16]

It is this total forgetfulness of self in living close to God that Mary regards as the perfection of poverty. Mary MacKillop was careful to distinguish between material poverty and being 'truly poor in spirit', which is to be stripped of human desires, so that one is not always wanting this and wanting that. Most people today are looking out for themselves, not forgetting about themselves. We tend to measure people by what they have rather than by who they are. Mary knew how difficult it is to live 'self-forgetfully'. She goes into a person's motives for any trace of deception:

> Let us watch carefully over the desires and motions of our hearts, for often we may appear in the eyes of creatures to observe poverty whilst the pure searching eye of our Divine Spouse finds not a shadow even of that virtue in our hearts.[17]

One can appear poor while, in one's heart, there is no humility or self-forgetfulness. The Beatitudes tell us that to be poor in spirit is to be blessed or happy, for it is to have the Kingdom of Heaven, which is another way of saying that those who are poor in spirit know the nearness of God. Poverty, in the sense of leaning on God, was the spirit of the Institute. There is a mutuality in the concept of leaning such that, when I lean, God supports. The concept of poor in spirit also has a paradoxical mutuality: when I know that I have nothing then I know God provides everything.

There are two concepts that Mary MacKillop associated with spiritual poverty: dependence and detachment. Poverty makes a person dependent. Spiritual poverty makes a person realise that she is dependent on God. At the same time, a person is detached because she chooses not to have any attachments, so that she can dwell more fully on her dependence on God. What does Mary teach us about the spirituality of poverty and her views on the associated concepts of dependence and detachment? It is spiritual poverty about which she was most concerned. She speaks of poverty of spirit as 'this sweet hidden treasure'. It was what the Sisters had come into Religious life to find. How does Mary MacKillop understand the connection between poverty and dependence and poverty and detachment?

## Poverty and Dependence upon God

For Mary, dependence on God was just as important for poverty as having no property, no possessions and no money. It was the ultimate objective of the Sisters' vow of poverty – to realise their dependence upon God. Their lives were to resemble the lives of the disciples. Jesus said, 'Take no gold or silver or copper in your belts, no bag for your journey' (Matt. 10:10). The Sisters were to be poor with the poor Christ, not only materially poor, but entirely poor before God, the Father. Mother Mary recognised the challenge this presents. The Sisters had to empty themselves (*kenosis*) in order to realise their poverty of spirit. She wrote to the Sisters:

> The true Sister of St Joseph does not study herself but her work. She has left self outside the Convent. Have you all

done this, or have you been in danger of taking back from God the offering you made of yourself when you became His Spouse? ... I want my darling Sisters ... to be what they are intended to be – God's ministering visible angels on earth, striving in visible form to imitate the pure spirits who serve him without any thought of aught but His slightest wish.[18]

Self-emptying and coming to the end of oneself is the sure way to know that, in the providence of God, one is not poor but rich. This is the paradox of being poor in spirit.

Dependence on God and homelessness are connected in Mary's spirituality.

A saying of Jesus' that Mary loved was:

The foxes have their holes and the birds of the air their nests, but the Son of Man has nowhere to lay his head.[19]

It is a statement that speaks of being poor and totally dependent on God. But at the same time it is a reminder to the Sisters that they, like Christ, do not own any property of their own. Sandra Schneiders speaks of the implications of owning one's own home:

Perhaps nothing in our culture is as symbolic of self-sufficiency as 'owning one's own home'. It is a way of describing someone who is financially secure and independent.[20]

Like Jesus, the Sisters were to be homeless, not in the sense of being destitute, for he relied on his friends to provide him with a home when he needed it, such as Peter's house at Capernaum. But he was dependent on his friends to share what they had with him. The Sisters were also to share. The *Constitutions* say 'we see that sharing is an essential element of our poverty'. But it does require a change of attitude from 'It's mine' to 'It's ours', which is not always easy.

Today we need to find the simplicity of poverty, by living close enough to the limits of our resources so that we can rely on God's providence and appreciate the beauty of life. Mary rested in the assurance of God's providence and she found much in life that was beautiful. Poverty is very much a matter of balance, between what we need and what we can give to those in greater need than ourselves. In order to find that balance, we have to depend on God. We are still trying to live as Mary MacKillop would have wished her Sisters to live, with the simplicity of Jesus and with an awareness of what we have to give to the poor. However, for Mary, dependence on God was the bright side of poverty. To know that one is completely and utterly dependent on God is to know that one is blessed.

## Poverty and Detachment

A final way of understanding spiritual poverty is to be detached and to be without attachments. Mary wrote a letter to the Sisters from Rome on 12 April 1874, which she devoted to the subject of 'true religious detachment'.

She says, almost in fun to begin with:

> Some of you may smile and think this is a singular subject for a letter, well smile away but listen at the same time.[21]

By 'detached', Mary did not mean aloof, or distanced from what was going on. She meant that the Sisters were not to be governed by their desires. Being detached was no easy matter. It required discipline to be free from the push and pull of desire. Detachment came with experience, which many of the early Sisters were too young to have. They owe it to Jesus to have no attachments and to allow him to fill their hearts. He has almost emptied himself of his graces for their benefit, Mary tells them. If he has done this for love of them, they must empty themselves of all their attachments and divided affections to show their love for him. This emptying of themselves may be painful but it is spiritual poverty, the poverty they chose when they took their vow of poverty.

It was St Joseph's detachment that Mary particularly wished the Sisters to admire and emulate. His detachment was 'the complete abnegation of his heart'. There was no thought of what he himself might have wanted. His sole concern was for the Virgin Mary and the child Jesus, which was the mission God had given him. That was how it was to be for the Sisters as well. They were to be completely immersed in their mission – teaching the children of the poor with no thought of what they might want for themselves.

Mary knew that without detachment the Sisters would be torn apart by love of self and love of God. She urged them not to have any attachments, otherwise they would 'only have the divided affection of their hearts' to offer to Christ. Jesus had a place in their hearts but it was not always first place. In her letter on religious detachment, Mary wrote:

> He (Jesus) showed the restless activity of their minds, the slothful indifference with which they discharged their various occupations. They professed to love him and many had the reputation of doing so … They only loved him with their lips and outward manner, that their hearts were so full of self and self-seeking …[22]

The poverty of detachment was the hardest form of poverty. It was the antidote to possessiveness. It went against nature and all their inclinations. But it had great rewards as far as Mary was concerned. It would bring the Institute and their communities unity and peace, and put an end to those 'murmurings' that Mary hated so much.

It was Mary who wrote to the Sisters about living frugally, with dependence on God and detachment. I find detachment a rather cold and distancing virtue, although I am sure Mother Mary did not mean it to be. Is attachment as full of self and self-seeking as she suggests? One may be attached to something worthy that would not detract from one's love of Christ. Diarmuid O'Murchu speaks of the 'spirituality of attachment', by which he means an attachment to the sacredness of simple things. It is the sacred loveliness of an African violet or the rare flower of a cactus to which we have a brief attachment, for their beauty that can cheer poverty with gratitude. Within the context of detachment there needs to be a place for attachment. I believe that Mother Mary would agree. There must have been many occasions when the smile of a poor, ragged child brought to her heart a sacred moment of love. We need to find a balance between being detached and having spiritual attachments that are consistent with poverty.

## Poverty – the Challenge

What can we learn from Mary and Julian about poverty? The no ownership aspect of poverty, which Mary subscribed to for only a relatively short time, was a negative approach. It would encourage humility to own nothing and it would promote non-possessiveness; but the adamant way in which Julian insisted on no ownership of any kind was almost irresponsible. Ownership requires responsibility, and a certain maturity that were being denied to the Sisters.

Mary and Julian had no hesitation in asking the Sisters to do without. The challenge there is that we can sometimes give but not so as to do without ourselves. We have enough to give and still have sufficient for ourselves. Unless we have a sense of really going without ourselves, we have not encountered poverty.

It has become clear that poverty in Religious life has changed its emphasis from no ownership and not having enough money, to living simply with an awareness of those who do not have what we have and an endeavour for a more just distribution of God's gifts. Religious life has an air of simplicity about it but it is the living of simplicity in a community that remains difficult.

> With all the pressures to buy this and have that, it is difficult to be satisfied with having just enough to be generous and caring.[23]

Giving to those in need is a challenge to the vow of poverty. We have to decide how much to give to be generous and caring and still have enough for ourselves. Mary MacKillop was always giving to those in need, whether she had enough for herself or not. She was known to give her dinner to a poor man who came to the door as they were sitting down to a meal. Another challenge is to resist the pressures that we constantly live with. To be able to overcome the temptation to buy more than we need is ever present.

In the recent past, however, these were not challenges for the Sisters, because they had virtually nothing to give, nor was there any danger of buying more than they needed. This is what one Sister told me of how she had experienced poverty:

> Poverty was very real in my own Religious life up until about 1970. I lived mostly in country convents where we relied solely on school fees (very little!) and whatever money the Parish could afford. We received vegetables, sometimes meat, eggs, poultry from the people and we lived frugally. A trip to Sydney was only in cases of dire necessity or for Retreat and we had to go without for the rest of the year because of the expense of fares. We had no car so we had to 'beg' someone to drive us into the nearest town … and how I hated that! We wasted *nothing*.[24]

This was genuinely living with poverty, as Mary MacKillop would have understood it. Lack of money meant that they were dependent on the generosity of others for their food and transport. It involved sharing between laity and Religious. They were the poor ones in need. Religious today need to set an example by reducing their wants and limiting their desires. Religious do not own anything themselves and yet their vow of poverty means everything is theirs. It challenges us to be in touch with the disadvantaged and how we can live to be of service to them. We are no longer the poorest of the poor but we are called to be with them in whatever hardships they are enduring.

The poor are not just those who do not have sufficient money. They are anyone who does not have what they have a right to: food, adequate housing and education. Mary MacKillop knew that God was present in the ordinary things of life and in every event. God was in every encounter and in whatever happened. God was close to her in her endeavour to help the poor and to bring relief wherever it was needed. It was her own experience of poverty that made her dream of reaching out to poor children who longed to know they mattered.

The challenge Mary gives to us is to live simple, balanced lives. We need to find a balance between what we have to give to the marginalised in our world and what we can use for ourselves; a balance between the needs of the earth and our own unnecessary comforts. It is a balance for each person to achieve in their own life, either with community or on their own. One cannot live well, trying to find a balance, without prayer.

# 6

## Mary MacKillop's Heart and the Sacred Heart

*... on the scales of God only hearts have any weight.*
Karl Rahner

When I speak of Mary MacKillop's heart, I am not thinking of her physiological heart but of her loving response to life, God and Jesus Christ. Just as, when I speak about the Sacred Heart of Jesus, I am thinking of his love for each one of us. The Sacred Heart is symbolic of the love that is at the 'heart' of life. The Sacred Heart is essentially a pierced heart from which love pours forth. Mary's heart was similarly pierced, not by a soldier's spear but by the cruel barbs of bishops. Mary was able to rise above and forgive the opposition she endured because she had found the truth of the Sacred Heart as the ground of her life.

Devotions to the Sacred Heart today are not as popular as they were in Mary MacKillop's time. Many have lapsed altogether. That is not necessarily a bad thing because much of what was done in the name of the Sacred Heart was a matter of externals – banners, badges, medals and pictures. Many of the pictures would be regarded as unacceptably sentimental today. Although Mary mentioned the Sacred Heart frequently in her letters, and had a great devotion to the Heart of Jesus, she did not specially talk about Devotions to the Sacred Heart, probably because they were taken for granted. One could say that she lived in an era of Sacred Heart spirituality. Today we speak more about the Holy Spirit, Pentecost and the love of God. In the second half of the nineteenth century people talked, lived and breathed devotion to the Sacred Heart. It is not so today; for better or for worse we have moved on. Today we live in an intellectual, technological, rational era. There is no real understanding of the spiritual significance of heart, never mind the Heart of Jesus. In the present-day's slick communications culture, the symbol of a heart is used for anything a person likes, from lollies to a favourite breed of dog or a place. The heart has been trivialised and trashed by advertising.

Can Mary help us to redirect our spirituality to engage more with the Heart of Jesus? I believe her own heart will lead us to a deeper understanding of a spirituality of the Sacred Heart that we can apply to life today.

For Mary, the Sacred Heart entered into every department of life. It guided her in her mission to teach poor children. It was to the loving Heart of Jesus that she prayed. The only pilgrimage she ever went on was to Paray-le-Monial in honour of the Sacred Heart. When she wanted to encourage the Sisters she told them to go to the Sacred Heart in prayer. It was the foundation of her life and the life of the Institute. An understanding of the Sacred Heart is essential for understanding her spirituality.

In this chapter, I shall first of all examine how the Sacred Heart came to have the importance it had in Mary MacKillop's time. Secondly, I am going to look at the meaning of the words sacred and heart. Thirdly, I shall discuss her spirituality in relation to the Sacred Heart. How does it connect with the mission of the Institute? How does pilgrimage throw light on her spirituality? What was the special encouragement that she felt the Sacred Heart would give her Sisters? I shall spend some time on her reflection on the Sacred Heart as an abyss. Lastly, I shall look at how Mary MacKillop's spirituality of the Sacred Heart shares some similarities with Karl Rahner's spirituality of the Pierced Heart, which is very relevant for today.

## Why the Sacred Heart was so Important in the Time of Mary MacKillop

Devotions to the Sacred Heart go back to St Margaret Mary Alacoque, a Visitation nun (1647–1757). Jesus appeared to her several times between 1673 and 1675, and made promises to her for those who practised the Devotions. The practice of honouring the Heart of Jesus is a development of his sacred humanity and of his love for sinners that inspires a response 'like a river in full flood, sweeping away all obstacles'.[1]

From the time of Pope Clement XIII (1699–1709), great attention was given to the Sacred Heart. Ninety years after Margaret Mary Alacoque's death, Pius IX commanded that the Feast of the Most Sacred Heart be extended to the whole Church. Leo XIII (1810–1903) consecrated the whole world to the Sacred Heart. Pope Pius XII completed the work of his predecessors. He wrote:

> Various projects conducive to fostering the devotion … have happily arisen … in particular the extremely fervent expressions of piety which are the fruit of the Sodality of the Apostleship of Prayer, under whose aegis, principally families, colleges, situations, and at times even whole nations, have been consecrated to the Most Sacred Heart of Jesus.[2]

The Sisters of St Joseph were founded at a time when devotion to the Sacred Heart was surging forward to counter the heresy of Jansenism, which held that people were too sinful to have the Eucharist, except very occasionally. This is contrary to the teaching of the Sacred Heart of Jesus, since it denies people the expression of their love in the Eucharist as a return for Jesus' sacrifice for us. Mary did not speak or write publicly to the Sisters about the heresy. She was too much in love with the Heart of Jesus to be concerned about the circumstances that had brought the Sacred Heart into such prominence.

The Sacred Heart today does not have the spiritual significance that it had in the nineteenth century, when there was a resurgence of Devotions to combat Jansenism. Since Vatican II, which stressed the importance of the Eucharist as our daily worship, there has been a decline in Sacred Heart Devotions. Catholics have rightly believed that nothing can or should take the place of the Eucharist.

The devotion of the two founders of the Sisters of St Joseph to the Sacred Heart is shown in the name they gave to the Institute.

The name originally given to the Institute was Sisters of St Joseph of the Sacred Heart. However, Sisters of St Joseph of the *Most* Sacred Heart of Jesus is what the Institute has sometimes been called, as recently as the 1960s. If one reads the various encyclicals of the Sacred Heart that have used the phrase 'Most Sacred Heart', it is understandable why the title of the Congregation also changed. When the Institute was constituted into a Regular Congregation (25 July 1888), the title used in the Decree was Sisters of St Joseph of the Sacred Heart of Jesus. As far as I know, to Mary, the title was the simplest one, as it is today: Sisters of St Joseph of the Sacred Heart. The fact that the name has changed is indicative of the new and developing status of the Institute. When it became a Regular Congregation that meant it was no longer under diocesan control of the Bishop, but was under the jurisdiction of Rome.

We have lost the way to the Sacred Heart today. It was obviously important to Mary, but not for us in the changed world of today. However, something needs to be reclaimed for Josephite life in the present. I am not saying that Devotions to the Sacred Heart need to be stepped up and promoted, but the need for a spirituality of the Sacred Heart should not be lost sight of. The Sacred Heart still has a formative place in the charism and mission of the Congregation and for today's world. The Sacred Heart is still a vibrant element in the name of the Congregation – not a lame tailpiece!

## The Meaning of Sacred and Heart for Mary MacKillop

The phrase 'Sacred Heart' is closely associated with another word, 'devotion'. Devotion is a very deeply held love and respect for a person. In a religious context, it is a reverently-held love for the person of Jesus that is often expressed by the word 'veneration'. We revere the Sacred Heart of Jesus.

Mary MacKillop had a great devotion to the Sacred Heart. She knew, in the words of Karl Rahner, that 'the centre of the whole world and of all truth is a heart, a burning heart'[3]. The flames indicate the intensity of that Heart's love. In depictions of the Sacred Heart, the flames are shown as blazing out of the Heart of Jesus, consuming it and not able to be contained. They are a symbol of his inestimable love for the world.

What does the word 'sacred' mean to Mary? Apart from the phrase 'Sacred Heart', which she uses over thirty times in the book of her *Circulars*,[4] Mary does not use the word 'sacred' very much, if at all. Part of the reason for this may be that her letters tend to be practical. But it is also a word that she reserved for Heart. It is the Heart of Jesus that she wants to venerate and wants her Sisters to revere and honour with Sacred. Something is sacred when a person dedicates themselves to it. 'Sacred' is a connecting word. It connects precious times in a person's life with the Heart of Jesus – when a Sister dedicates herself by taking vows, when she celebrates twenty five years, fifty years, and more, of dedicated service, and other special times. They are sacred through the love of the Heart of Jesus.

The word 'heart' needs to be reclaimed from a heap of words that have lost their original meanings and are thought to be not worth talking about (for example, 'gay'). 'Heart' nowadays means whatever a person likes. 'Heart' is no longer a sacred word. According to Karl Rahner,[5] 'heart' is a primordial word. Primordial means first or prime order or level. 'Heart' essentially belongs to humanity and human life. Thus, the heart is the basis of what it is to be human. The Heart of Jesus is part of the mystery of the God-person he was. The word 'heart' takes us beyond emotion and romantic love to a heart, any heart, that is lovingly united to the pierced Heart of Jesus. Only when we know the full weight of the word 'heart', as meaning a bridge of love binding the human and eternity together, can we begin to understand why 'heart' is a sacred word. 'On the scales of God only hearts have any weight.'[6] It is the piercing of his heart that reveals how much Christ loved us. The words 'Sacred Heart' need to be redeemed from silence by adoration. It is the apex of mystery.

'Heart' can either be used in a symbolic sense or a physiological sense. Mary had a biblical concept of heart that was symbolic. The heart was the hidden ground of a person's being, from which flowed the choices and motives that shape the identity and integrity of a person. Proverbs tells us to 'Keep watch over your heart since here are the wellsprings of life'.[7] This text shows clearly the creative, primordial sense of heart as the wellspring of life. The Heart and Person of Jesus were one and the same for Mary. The heart is the centre of his Person and the depths of his love for us. She wrote: 'It was thus the tender and loving heart of my Jesus who spoke to me'.[8] She understood the Heart of Jesus as the source of his dispositions and his total self-giving to the Will of God. She believed that, through veneration of the Sacred Heart, her Sisters would be empowered to have the disposition of being generously open and self-giving to the Will of God.

The Sacred Heart is particularly symbolic of unity for Mary. The heart is a natural symbol of unity. Just as the blood in different blood vessels, veins, arteries and capillaries all flows through the heart in the one bloodstream, so the Heart of Jesus is a centre of unity for the Church and society, religious communities and families. It is an open, inclusive Heart, welcoming all, unifying and making one. The unity of the Institute was of prime importance to Mary. 'In our unity under God lies our strength,'[9] she wrote. The Heart of Jesus was the deep centre of unity, both the unity of a Sister's integrity and the unity of a community, which she saw as being closely connected. The unity that she is speaking of is what she calls 'unity under God', springing up from the Heart of Christ, as the loving centre of Religious life. It is a unity that is directed by God. As such, it is not static unity which is really only uniformity or conformity. Unity under God is dynamic and it is our strength. Our hearts need to be recharged from the Heart of Jesus, so that a wellspring of love can go out to the world from religious communities.

## Mary MacKillop's Spirituality of the Sacred Heart

Her spirituality of the Sacred Heart embraced the mystery of Jesus' life participating in her life and the lives of her Sisters. Mary

MacKillop and every Sister took their vows in honour of the Sacred Heart as well as out of love of Joseph, John the Baptist and the Virgin Mary. I believe we still need a spirituality of the Sacred Heart. The Heart – our hearts and the Heart of Jesus – is the mainspring of the Church's mission. If they do not reach out to others in love, our hearts stagnate and grow introverted.

Mary constantly spoke about the Sacred Heart to her Sisters. It was a language that had special significance for them, which it does not have today. Her spirituality is deeply rooted in the Sacred Heart. Daniel Lyne explains very well how the Sacred Heart is a symbol of her spirituality:

> If a symbol were to be chosen to enshrine the spirituality of Mary as centring around the Fatherhood of God, loving adherence to His Will, expressed in a life characterised by Cross and poverty – the symbol enshrining it all would be that of the Heart of Jesus as a symbol of love.[10]

Mary MacKillop saw the Heart of Jesus as being able to blend into one all the multiplicity and complexity of Religious life, so that from the inmost unity a channel for the love of his Heart to flow out into the world would be formed. All the symbolism of the Sacred Heart – the flames, the pierced heart, the thorns, all depicting the inestimable love of Jesus revealed in the Passion – is recalled in the liturgy of the Eucharist through the symbol of the Cross.

Her spirituality of the Sacred Heart spreads into every area of Religious life – doctrine, discipline, the Eucharist, work and mission, pilgrimage and prayer. Every aspect of her life was grounded on love; that is to say, on the Sacred Heart.

## Doctrine

Her teaching was mainly concerned with the Will of God, the Cross and our attitude to the Cross and poverty. The Fatherhood of God and union with his Will are the Christological foundations of her spirituality. Daniel Lyne explains for us:

For Mary MacKillop this Christological emphasis seems to be expressed predominantly in the lived experience of Cross and poverty.[11]

Mary was very conscious of the sufferings of Jesus and of her need to feel that she was suffering with him. The Sacred Heart is always a suffering heart. We have pierced it and it suffers out of love for us. In turn we try to love the Sacred Heart to make some reparation for the little love we have to give him. Mary understands only too well how the Sisters want to avoid their crosses. She writes to the Sisters:

> A little cross or contradiction comes, and away with all our good resolutions; we become cowards.[12]

She frequently told her Sisters to go to the Sacred Heart in prayer for the unity and charity that they needed in their communities. She taught them the importance of living together in unity because it reflected the love of the Heart of Jesus. They were to think of themselves as Sisters of the Sacred Heart as much as Sisters of St Joseph. She wrote to them:

> Would that I could tell you how much I long for a true spirit of charity and unity amongst you ... I must ask you to go to the Sacred Heart of Jesus.[13]

Again she writes to the Sisters:

> Next month will be the one of the Sacred Heart. Let us all entreat that generous Heart to give us some of its own sweet spirit of love ...[14]

In both these quotes from her correspondence she is urging the Sisters to be more intimate with the Sacred Heart. She knows that it is intimacy with the Sacred Heart through prayer that will make them all that she desires and, especially, to be united with Jesus. This is how they will be able to do the Will of God willingly and lovingly. We need to ask ourselves how intimate we are with Jesus. How far do we stretch out to help the poor out of sheer love?

## Discipline

Mary was not a disciplinarian but she had a sense of what was required if Sisters were to live happy lives together. Obedience was the key to genuinely happy communities. At a practical level, Sisters were to refrain from the temptation of criticising others, since this lack of discipline would grieve the Heart of Jesus. Mary wrote:

> You must know, dear ones ... how often deviations from obedience in some matters were made, how often criticism and murmurings were indulged in.[15]

She concludes her letter by saying, 'if the spirit of criticism is indulged in then goodbye to improvement'. Criticism was high on her list of what had to be eradicated. It was contrary to humility, charity, gentleness and caring for others. Criticism was often against Sisters who were in authority and vulnerable to those who mistakenly thought they knew better. How wounded the Heart of Jesus would have been to see a community so disunified.

Mary MacKillop saw the life of the Institute and its spiritual wellbeing as depending upon the Sisters living together in the Heart of Jesus, and not from their own personal and limited resources of love. It was the Sacred Heart that would achieve unity in communities and within the Institute. In one of her *Circulars* to the Sisters, she wrote:

> I often speak of this unity which should reign among us, as it is the bond that will ever keep us dear to the Sacred Heart.[16]

She also wrote to the Sisters about the need to forgive and be reunited:

> Remember now goodbye forever to old sores and for the future let us live and love in the charity of the Sacred Heart.[17]

Criticism and words that are not spoken in love are still the reasons for unhappy communities today. Disagreement and disunity come from deeply sown seeds of criticism that have been allowed to take root in someone's heart, leading to exaggeration and discontent. Mary MacKillop knew the human heart and loved it with all its foibles.

## The Eucharist

It is clear that Mary valued the Eucharist highly. In the *Positio,* vol. III, it is stated of her:

> Christ the Redeemer in the Eucharistic Sacrament was her life. His Sacred Heart was the centre of her thinking and her affections. It was there that she found inspiration and solace, strength to suffer and courage to persevere.[18]

She had a special devotion to the Heart of Christ in his Eucharistic presence.

Since Vatican II, we speak of the Eucharist as the pinnacle of worship and sacramental life. The Eucharist was also of great significance to Mary, who encouraged her Sisters to take the blessed Sacrament often.

She had some very human views about the Eucharist that are also spiritual, three in particular. Firstly, she speaks of Jesus as a Religious. She writes:

> Our blessed Lord for love of our souls, dwells with us as a religious in our convent but the most perfect religious that there ever was or will be.[19]

The Sacred Heart was present in the Eucharist to Mary through the Real Presence. But Jesus was present to her and the Sisters in a unique way in the Blessed Sacrament, as a Religious. There was special significance for a Religious in the total self-giving love of the Heart of Jesus in the Eucharist – his selfless anonymity and availability for all in the Bread and the Wine – and that was how a Sister should see herself: as anonymous and available for all. Mary makes the Sacred Heart relevant to the Sisters. An encounter with Jesus as a Religious in the Eucharist would inspire and nurture the unity that Mary recognised as vital to effective mission.

Secondly, she thinks of Jesus as being lonely in the tabernacle:

> Who so poor as our blessed Lord in the cold lonely prison
> of the tabernacle? What religious could consent to dwell
> thus in a cell for love of souls?[20]

The image of the Lord, cold and in a lonely prison for love of
them, would stir the Sisters' hearts and encourage them to go and
visit him either on their own for prayer or for Eucharist. When she
says, 'What religious could consent to dwell thus in a cell?' she is
challenging the Sisters to put themselves in the place of Jesus.
Mary is addressing a blind spot in the Eucharist that is still with us
today. We see Christ's body being broken but seldom see that we
ourselves are in the position of being broken and distributed for
the needs of the world.

Thirdly, she thinks of how he is treated as bread. She writes:

> (it is) lifted from place to place and in all things subject to
> His creatures.[21]

Again, Mary asks the question that she has already asked in relation
to living in a cold and lonely cell:

> Can we consent to be treated as Jesus is, and be like him, as
> a mere nothing in the hands of creatures?[22]

'… subject to His creatures,' powerless and having no freedom,
like a piece of bread for the nourishment of all. No Religious
would consent to be nothing more than ubiquitous bread, passed
from hand to hand. Yet it is the nature of the Sacred Heart, its
humility, its willingness to suffer and its desire to be available for all
that shows the depths and degree of its love.

Mary would have recognised the Heart of Jesus in the Eucharist
as a symbol of an inexhaustible charity towards all. She had a very
perceptive understanding of hearts being made *one* in the Heart of
Christ. His Heart is large enough to hold all our hearts. She knew
in her heart what we probably only acknowledge with our minds:
that the Heart of Jesus in his Eucharistic presence is the dynamic
factor that breaks open our hearts to include the poor.

## Work and Mission

Mary MacKillop's spirituality of the Sacred Heart was practical, not pious. The Sacred Heart was a source of strength and great encouragement to the early Sisters and their founder in their work of educating poor children. In 1870, when the Sisters first went to Queensland, she wrote to Julian Tenison Woods:

> Thank God, they (the Sisters) are very happy, and how can they be otherwise, when they see so much that they may try to do for the love of the Sacred Heart.[23]

It was not long, however, until they encountered a difficulty over a Government grant for education. The policy of the Brisbane Diocese was to accept Government grants, but there were conditions attaching to them which included restrictions on religious instruction. Mary refused the grant because to accept would have been contrary to the Josephite Rule. But she had to face opposition from the Bishop. In a letter, she used the Sacred Heart as an argument to support her case against accepting Government grants:

> Sisters of St Joseph of the Sacred Heart ... we must be true to it (the Sacred Heart). We must lean on it and not on the world – its enemy. We never, never can be connected with any secular Board of Education, even granted that a free use of our religious principles might be allowed, we must be left free to appoint our own teachers and adhere strictly to our own system – otherwise endless evils would ensue and the work of the Sacred Heart would not go on. Were we to depart in the least from this, the whole would fail – It would cease to be God's work.[24]

The mission of the Sisters was to teach poor children – to give them very basic education and a grounding in the Catholic Faith. This was an outreach of the love of the Sacred Heart for the poor and, as such, it could not be compromised. To accept money from the Government would entitle them to prescribe what would be taught and who would teach. Mary could see that it would jeopardise the entire mission. The Sacred Heart was the foundation of the work of the Institute. It was the needs of the children that mattered, not satisfying Government regulations. The Sacred Heart gave her the courage to stand up for what she believed.

She urged the Sisters to lean on the Sacred Heart, to trust it and to be filled with its spirit of total commitment to the poor.

By focusing on the Sacred Heart, Mary was certain that they would be true to the objectives of the Institute to living their vow of poverty and loving the poor children and their families.

## *Pilgrimage*

As far as we know, Mary only went on one pilgrimage, in May 1873, during her travels in Europe. She joined the Jubilee Pilgrimage from London to Paray-le-Monial in France (the place where a vision of Jesus had appeared to St Margaret Mary Alacoque). It was the first time such a pilgrimage in honour of the Sacred Heart had gone from England. It was a great witness to the Catholic Church. Mary described it as 'one grand act of devotion to the Sacred Heart'. It was also in honour of the sanctity of family life, at a time when Catholics in Britain found it difficult to get employment. Mary MacKillop recognised that it was a historic moment that she very much wanted to be part of. Joining the pilgrimage must have been an exhilarating experience, in which Catholics from all over Britain and probably other parts of the world were able to come together in a unified witness to the power of the love of Jesus in their lives, and to go to behold the place where Christ had appeared.

Mary would have rejoiced because it was an opportunity to witness to the importance to her of the Sacred Heart. She went in the interests of the Institute, and representing the Sisters of St Joseph of the Sacred Heart, and to petition the Sacred Heart for the Catholics of Australia.

She stayed with the nuns of the Visitation in Paray-le-Monial and wrote to her Sisters in Adelaide that, when she left, they gave her a paper of affiliation to their community for the Institute. She said:

> When you know that theirs was the first convent in which the month of the Sacred Heart was kept you will not wonder at the joy with which I found myself amongst them.[25]

Clearly she felt that being affiliated to their community was an honour for the Institute. The month of the Sacred Heart (June) was important to her as a special time of devotion. To have stayed in the convent, where in a sense the Devotion had all started two hundred years earlier, gave her great joy. Back in Australia she had started something too – not a devotion but something that was dedicated to, and in honour of, the Sacred Heart – an Institute for the education of poor children.

Pilgrimage connects with spirituality because it is a time when pilgrims draw closer to God and when their hearts are full of the mercy and love of God. That was so for Mary. On her return to London she wrote to her Sisters:

> How dear our individual souls are to the Sacred Heart, and how It loves to shelter ALL there in one great universal bond of love … May that most gracious of all hearts teach you what I wish to say but cannot express.[26]

It had been a spiritual experience for her that she wished to share with the Sisters as far as she possibly could, but she found it difficult to express the 'universal bond of love' that the pilgrimage had evoked for her.

Her spirituality of the Sacred Heart entered into every aspect of her life, where the Cross and poverty were present. It is hard for us to apprehend the pain she knew in her life, through opposition and ill-health and sheer hardship. Yet the Heart of Jesus was the symbol of love that enabled her to bear all the pain gladly for love of her Lord.

## Prayer

Mary MacKillop knew that the deep love and inmost unity needed for Religious life, can only be experienced through an encounter in prayer with the Heart of Jesus. An encounter is more than a superficial meeting, like the collision of two billiard balls. A true encounter is an in-depth, life-changing experience. Mary knew it must engage her Sisters' attention at a deep level of reflection and prayer. That was why she urged them to go to the Sacred Heart in prayer. Henri Nouwen explains a deep encounter with God:

> Prayer is standing in the presence of God with the mind in the heart. That is at the point of our being where there are no divisions or distinctions and where we are totally one. There God's spirit dwells and there the great encounter takes place. There heart speaks to heart because there we stand before the face of the Lord, all-seeing within us.[27]

Henri Nouwen uses a significant phrase: 'the mind in the heart'. Ideas without the heart or charity are the source of division. Our minds work by dividing things up and putting them into categories. Only when the mind is subject to the heart, reigned into the heart, are we free to become involved in divine recreative love and compassion. Mary MacKillop saw an encounter with the Heart of Jesus as the centre of the Sisters' unity. But she also saw that the unity would be costly. She knew their hearts needed to enter into the pierced Heart of Christ so that they could look with the love of his Heart on the tragic dysfunctional families and the disunity in society and the world.

## The Sacred Heart – an Abyss

Mary did not write her reflection on the Sacred Heart until near the end of her life, just two years before she died. She did not say what the Sacred Heart meant to her, or what it symbolised for her, until 21 May 1907.

She told us that the Sacred Heart is a 'deep abyss', deep enough and large enough for her to creep into, where she can settle and be at home like a dove in the cleft of a rock. She crept into a Heart of Love, where she felt her own heart was at home and no longer 'passion-tossed'. The Sacred Heart is an endless, fathomless chasm of steep love within her. It is not an inner heart-room, as it would have been for St Teresa of Avila, but an unconfined, wide-open space, like the bush with all its attractions for her, deep down within her. She felt secure there and her soul was at peace in the stillness. The Sacred Heart was a refuge from the coldness of the world, a 'place' where she could be alone with God, where she and God were completely one. It is a beautiful moment of contemplation that Mary wrote about to share with her Sisters:

> Its love makes the world a desert. When storms rage, when persecutions or dangers threaten, I quietly creep into its deep abyss.[28]

What made her choose the word abyss? Abyss may suggest desolation or forsakenness but as Mary uses it, it means neither. The abyss that is the Sacred Heart is a welcoming, spacious place that invites her to enter an eternal peace, where hearts meld and the weary, disappointed soul finds where she belongs. The abyss is full of sacred yearning. It is the response of her heart to the Sacred Heart.

The Sacred Heart was not a physiological heart. It was a state of being where she responded to the appeal of the love of God for her with her own heart. She wrote with all the passion of the Song of Songs:

> With the burning appeal of the Sacred Heart came such a rushing of longing desire on my part to be its lover and its own true child.[29]

We all have these moments of being in love with Love. Mary speaks of a 'rushing of longing desire', which does not mean that she was deeply dissatisfied but rather that the rushing lifts her up to the point of fulfilment, so that she can say, with the writer of the

Song of Songs: 'I am my beloved's and my beloved is mine; he pastures his flock among the lilies'.[30] This is an expression of consummation and oneness.

It is a powerful appeal to her to be his lover and to bring back his straying children into the security of the Sacred Heart. But they are ungrateful. She writes that the Sacred Heart says: 'I make offers of love and am rejected … I will crave for your love until you give it completely to me'. The Heart of Jesus is helpless. It waits for someone to come who 'comprehends the breadth and length and height and depths of the love of Christ,' and will show gratitude.

In this reflection Mary expresses what she was not able to express after the pilgrimage to Paray-le-Monial. Her heart has overflowed with love – for her Sisters, and for the children she has taught and longed to bring to a true knowledge of God. The Sacred Heart is the love of her life and now she expresses the certainty that she is his lover too. 'Will you be my lover? Will you seek for happiness in me? Will you suffer me to teach you?' Running through the whole reflection there is the same mystical sentiment of the Song of Songs. There is no doubt Mary was in love with the Sacred Heart. She wrote:

> The beauty, the pity, and the generosity of the Sacred Heart in this loving appeal could not be resisted.[31]

The weary disappointed soul to whom the Sacred Heart was speaking may be Mary's, but the Sacred Heart was also disappointed with the response to its burning appeal. She had written the reflection for the Sisters and told them of the comfort she herself had derived from the Sacred Heart. It had always provided an escape from 'the cold and selfish world'. She wanted the appeal to 'come home to each one as I often feel it does to me'. It was the loving Heart of Jesus who went on appealing passionately but to an often ungrateful world and to those who are weary. Mary urges us to respond generously to the appeal of the Sacred Heart, feeling it kindling our hearts with its burning appeal. Words from the Song of Songs come to mind:

Many waters cannot quench love,
Neither can floods drown it. (8:7)


## The Need Today for a Spirituality of the Sacred Heart

Karl Rahner, who has written extensively on a spirituality of the
pierced Heart of Christ, is able to give a contemporary relevance
to the Sacred Heart, which speaks to the present troubles of a
world that has become tragically divided and insecure, 'ravaged by
heart suffering and strife of every kind', to use Sister Annice
Callahan's words. Karl Rahner's understanding of the Sacred Heart
is of a heart pierced by sin and suffering, and its own powerlessness
in the face of a world of agonising tumult. Mary MacKillop longed
for her Sisters to suffer willingly for all Christ's agony. She herself
knew what it was to suffer helplessly, physically and mentally,
which she did to make amends for Christ's suffering. Reparation
does not strike a chord with us today but identification with
Christ's suffering is something we have to be prepared for.

Another aspect of Rahner's spirituality of the Pierced Heart that
Mary would have understood is that our hearts need to be
transformed into the Heart of Jesus – a heart that is both pierced
and at rest. It is this Heart of Christ – opened for the world in
sacrificial love – which we encounter in Eucharist. We need to
open our own hearts to receive the Heart of Christ, so that we go
out from the Eucharistic table to birth the Heart of Jesus into the
world.

The Heart of Jesus loved with an unstoppable love that encom-
passed everything and everyone, even the thief on the Cross. The
all-inclusive, non-judgemental spirit of Love is the Josephite
charism that Sisters and Associates are called to live out in the
world. That is not easy in today's highly critical, judgemental
society.

Karl Rahner urges us, in *Unity – Love – Mystery*:

> Go forth from the heart and centre of your own being in
> order that you may find your own heart.[32]

Mary MacKillop went out from 'the heart and centre' of her being and she found her heart in ragged children and beggars who blessed her. Where shall we find our own hearts today?

I believe it is through the Eucharist that the Heart of Jesus still inspires us today. Eucharist is at the centre of a spirituality of the Heart of Christ that is needed more than ever in the world. Karl Rahner gives us the message of the pierced Heart of Jesus:

> He risked the adventure of a human heart until pierced by the sin of the world, it had flowed out, until it had suffered to the end on the Cross the uselessness and powerlessness of his love and had become thereby the eternal heart of the world.[33]

For Mary MacKillop, the Sacred Heart was the ground of her life. By understanding her spirituality of the Sacred Heart we can be led by her to a spirituality of the Heart of Christ that is relevant for today. It is not a 'lovey-dovey' love. It is a challenging love that comes from a heart that was pierced and bruised but, in spite of that, loved creatively and compassionately. Mary's heart drew strength to love by, in the words of Annice Callahan, 'entering into the attitudes and dispositions of the pierced heart of Jesus,' exposing her own vulnerability, by feeling distressed for those who hurt her, by never bearing a grudge against anyone. She invites us to take the same risk of loving totally no matter what life does to us. Are our hearts large enough to accept the challenge?

# 7

# Mary MacKillop, Ignatius Loyola and Obedience

*Obedience in its true Biblical sense is not about subjecting one's will to another, but utilising all our God-given resources to listen more deeply to divine wisdom, so that we can discern God's will more authentically – for ourselves and for God's creation.*

Diarmuid O'Murchu

The Evangelical Counsels are chastity, poverty and obedience. They have been regarded as Vows that form the gateway to Religious life. There have always been three but they have not always been considered to be equally significant. The emphasis has varied according to the culture. Mary MacKillop believed that obedience was a fundamental virtue and an important Vow, so much so that obedience had the force of law, as we shall see.

Religious life has changed over the years, as we can see from Sandra Schnieders' book, *Selling All*.[1] She discusses the names of the Evangelical Counsels, in particular chastity. She argues that 'consecrated celibacy' is preferable to 'chastity', and that it is the one essential vow for Religious life. She is partly brought to that conclusion because of the emphasis on sex in society today and the fact that those entering Religious life are probably experienced in, or at least knowledgable about, sex. 'Chastity', on the other hand, has a negative meaning of total abstinence and a history that goes back to the Middle Ages. There is no doubt that Religious life has changed. For one thing, obedience has lost the importance it had in the time of Mary MacKillop because we no longer understand what it means. The structures relating to authority have crumbled, with the result that obedience is a neglected virtue in society and in Religious life. It is time we resurrected it so that we are able to understand its meaning for Religious life today.

Even in society, 'obedience' and its cognates are words that are not much used. In general, 'obedient' tends to be a word that we apply to children. For example, 'Jane is an obedient girl' or 'Jane is a disobedient child'. What it means is that Jane either does as she is told or does not do as she is told. There really is no comparable use of the term for adults. Who has the right or authority to say to an adult: 'You are a disobedient man (or woman)'? Someone might say: 'You are not thinking straight'; but people generally think for themselves and decide whether they will do whatever it is or not. Authority – having the right to enforce obedience – is very lacking in society today. However, I am not concerned with obedience, or its absence, in our culture, but with the need for it in Religious life.

It is inevitable that obedience should raise the issue of authority. After the Chapter of 1995, the Sisters of St Joseph no longer had Superiors (Little Sisters) in many of their convents. This was done in the spirit of Vatican II, to help Sisters break out of spiritual infantilism, where they were always tending to look for someone else to take the lead. Communities today are democratic in the way they reach decisions. However, there is also a hierarchy of authority. In the first place, there is the Congregational Leader and her team and, in the second place, there are Provincial Leaders and their teams. Issues that would have been handled in communities by the Superior may now be dealt with either at Provincial or Congregational level, which is not always satisfactory.

We have to be clear that obedience does not mean just doing as you are told; that is simplistic. There is far more to obedience than that, which tends to bring to mind a soldier doing what is commanded rigidly. When a Religious says 'I vow to God obedience for my whole life', he or she does not mean 'I will do as I am told for the rest of my life'. The Latin derivation of obedience is *obedire*, which means to listen attentively. It all depends to whom one is listening, to a person or to God. But doing what one is told has nothing to do with the root meaning of obedience, although it may follow from the attentive listening.

## What Obedience Meant to Mary MacKillop

Obedience loomed large in Mary MacKillop's thinking. She saw it as the way to achieving unity and happiness within communities. She did not advocate obedience as an end in itself. It was always as a means to achieving the end of unity. But can it do so? Obedience has some hard connotations apart from doing as you are told: a lack of freedom, acquiescing rigidly, punishment if one disobeys, not getting one's own way. None of these was foremost in Mary MacKillop's mind. Obedience was a matter of offering oneself to God. It was a desire for God; an overwhelming desire. Of the vow of obedience she writes:

> This vow is a perfect offering of ourselves to God. In its perfection we ought to have no will of our own, but act entirely in obedience to Superiors.[2]

Obedience is another way of speaking of the Will of God. When she spoke of acting entirely in obedience to Superiors, Mary meant that we are to do the Will of God, as they ask, not submissively, nor because they have authority but purely out of love of God and as an offering of ourselves.

The key to understanding the importance Mary MacKillop placed on obedience is her esteem for Ignatius Loyola's spirituality, and especially his 'Letter on Obedience'.[3] At the first General Chapter Meeting of the Sisters of St Joseph of the Sacred Heart, on 19 March 1875, Ignatius' letter was referred to as being of the utmost importance. Paul Gardiner comments:

> Significantly the Letter on Obedience of Ignatius Loyola was taken up by the Chapter … and received among the laws of the Congregation. Mary MacKillop had learned well from her Jesuit advisors the lessons inculcated in the Epistle, and her conviction of its importance had influenced the Chapter's decision.[4]

Giving the 'Letter on Obedience' the status of a law of the Congregation would have meant among other things that every

Sister would have been obliged to read it or hear it being read and to have a copy of it. But it also gave obedience a formative standing for the Constitutions that was not accorded to either chastity or poverty, although the *raison d'etre* of the Sisters was to educate poor children. What were the lessons in the 'Letter on Obedience' that Mary MacKillop deemed to be of such importance? The main one was that obedience was fundamental to the secure foundation of the Congregation.

## St Ignatius' 'Letter on Obedience'

It was not an isolated reference at the Chapter to Ignatius' letter. Ten years later, in 1885, Mary MacKillop wrote:

> Be humble, prayerful, charitable and patient. I entreat you often to read St Ignatius' 'Epistle on Obedience'. It will tell you much that I wish, and serve as a guide at all times.[5]

Mary MacKillop had great faith in Ignatius. She could see in his remarks a wisdom that was peculiarly apposite for a Congregation that was just beginning and had so much to learn about authority, and how central to unity and peace the right attitude to authority was and still is. When she wrote 'Be humble, prayerful, charitable and patient,' it was obedience, she believed, that would help Sisters to acquire these other virtues. Ignatius quotes Saint Gregory: 'obedience is the only virtue which plants all the other virtues in the mind, and preserves them once they are planted'. Obedience is not just another virtue, like patience, charity and humility; it is at the root of a virtuous character. All the other virtues spring from it. We need to be rooted and grounded in obedience, that is, in an aptitude for listening attentively to God (*obedire*). Mary MacKillop knew that it is hard work planting and tending the beautiful trees of humility, prayerfulness, charity and patience, and that desiring the Will of God is the only way to fruitfulness.

In order to know what it was about Ignatius' letter that impressed Mary MacKillop so much, we need to probe into his letter. Underlying Ignatius' letter is a particular problem he faced of how a Religious responds to authority.[6] Even more important is understanding the meaning of obedience. The two matters are closely connected.

## How the Superior is Viewed by Ignatius

For Ignatius, the way the Superior is seen is of paramount importance. Obedience is not given to established rules but is concerned with relationships between Religious and Superiors. A Superior should not be looked upon as a human being who is liable to err but as the representative of Jesus Christ, for whose sake the Superior is obeyed. Ignatius tells us that the Superior should be looked on as 'the vicar of Christ our Lord', in other words as the voice of Christ. Thus we can see that there is more to obedience than doing as one is told. It is a matter of having faith in the Superior as the representative of Christ. A Superior is not to be obeyed because he or she is Prudent, or because of any other gift, but only because they stand in the place of God, who gives them their authority. Given that it is Christ who is to be obeyed, the Religious must recognise the Lord with utmost devotion and reverence. Obedience is not a matter of doing or executing something. It is a matter of an interior disposition of willingness and humility and love. At the same time, the Superior should be 'docile to God's Will in the exercise of his (or her) office' (Vatican II, p.476). He or she is to use his or her authority in the service of the community and be guided by God.

## How the Superior is Viewed by Mary MacKillop

Mary MacKillop followed Ignatius in seeing Superiors as Christ's representatives. She wrote:

> Ah, if we could only remember who it is that speaks to us through our Superiors through the humblest Little Sister in her convent, how easy every duty would be.[7]

By referring to the Superior as 'the humblest Little Sister', Mary MacKillop was concerned that a Superior should not be seen as in any way lording it over the Sisters in her community. There should be no fear of punishment. She was conscious of how hard it could be for a Sister to obey a Superior with humility. Her letters are full of reminders of the need to be charitable and humble, and warnings of the damage criticism and complaints can do. She wrote:

> You must know, dear ones, how often charity was thought-lessly wounded, how often deviations from obedience in little matters were made, how often criticisms and mur-murings were indulged in.[8]

The very expressive term, 'murmurings', is a favourite word of Mary MacKillop to describe the way her Sisters complained in subdued tones of discontent, and barely audible grumbling. But they were damaging to the unity of a community nonetheless, as she knew only too well.

For Mary MacKillop, a community consisted of Sisters and a Superior unlike today. Her belief was that all were equal. The position of Superior did not diminish the equality before God. Obedience is important to Mary MacKillop because it gave unity to communities. Unity is reached when each Sister and Superior is focusing on the Will of God, listening for God's voice (*obedire*) and not concerned with differences of opinion and disagreements, which are only appearances. The reality is obedience is straining to catch what God is saying in our hearts. Unity is a seamless robe. There are no joins or hang-ups. There is one mind in a commu-nity. Superior and Sisters are of one heart and mind. That is how Mary MacKillop saw an ideal community. She wrote:

> I often speak of the unity which should reign amongst us. This has much to do with obedience and humility.[9]

The theme of unity, community and obedience arises again and again in her *Circulars*. She wrote:

> Would that I could tell you how much I long for a true spirit of charity and unity amongst you ... Without unity

to and strict submission to your lawful superiors you
cannot long subsist. See then how careful you must be. In
our unity lies under God our strength.[10]

Mary MacKillop urged unity because she knew that without it
they would not last long. She may seem to favour Superiors but
she recognised that they were in a vulnerable position. They could
easily become targets for complaints. One murmuring Sister could
encourage others. There was only one Superior in a disaffected
community. Mary MacKillop was aware of their position:

> The Little Sister is often afraid of giving the obedience
> (command) lest it might be complied with in a reluctant
> manner and only be an occasion of disedification to the
> community.[11]

It mattered greatly how the Superior was regarded. She was called
Little Sister so that members of a community would care for her
and help her. She might make mistakes but there needed to be
great generosity of heart so that they could be overlooked and
forgiven. Unfortunately, it sometimes happened that a Superior
was conscious of her position and the power she had in a community, which was contrary to Jesus' example of washing the disciples' feet, where we see service is the true meaning of authority.

Mary MacKillop does not use the term 'authority' as much as
one might have expected. A Superior to her is not an authority
figure, that is, not someone who is there to enforce obedience. She
is there primarily to guide the Sisters under her care and to have
the gentleness of the Sacred Heart.

## The Meaning of Obedience

Ignatius comes to the meaning of obedience after he has considered the question of how the Superior is viewed, making sure that
the problem which gave rise to the letter in the first place has been
dealt with. On the other hand, he knows that obedience has been
misunderstood and that he needs to say something about its
meaning.

He identifies three degrees of obedience, or three steps, we might say, on the ladder to perfect obedience. Firstly, there is the sense of obedience we have already mentioned, 'the execution of what is commanded', although that does not merit the name of obedience, according to Ignatius. One can do as one is told mindlessly, without any thought of who it is that is asking and without really listening. This is not the deep obedience of willingness and humility that one vows to God and that Mary MacKillop speaks of. Ignatius dismisses it.

The second degree is to make the Superior's will one's own so that there is an interior agreement, whether one is willing the same thing or not. For example, the Superior tells me to shut the window and I want it left open. We are not willing (wanting) the same thing. Nevertheless, I shut it out of respect and consideration for her and because I wish to conform to her wishes, even although it means sacrificing my own wishes. I am making her will my own out of love for God, if not for the Superior. This is a good principle for convent life. One can make one's own the will of any other Sister in a community and be prepared to sacrifice one's own preference for the sake of unity.

The third degree, which involves a sister or a brother making an offering of their understandings, as well as their wills, is the highest and most costly degree of obedience. Ignatius wrote:

> Would to God that this obedience of the understanding were as much understood and practised as it is necessary to anyone living in religion and acceptable to God our Lord.

One's understanding is the intellectual part of the mind. It is concerned with judgments and opinions. We sometimes long to pass judgment on some matter. We love expressing our opinions. But obedience of the understanding requires a brother or a sister to submit his or her judgment to the judgment of the Superior. Ignatius explains why that is necessary by an example from astronomy, which is the study of the necessary, regular movements of stars and planets. One star is subject (obedient) to another and ordered and adjusted to the stronger movement of the other. It is the same with rational beings and obedience. There must be a similar subordination of the inferior to the Superior as there is with celestial bodies. This can only come about if the understanding and will of the Religious are in conformity with the Superior. Any attempt by a brother or sister to rely on their own judgment would be like a star or planet that went its own way and threw the system into disarray. It is a forceful way to stress the importance of obedience of the understanding.

Mary MacKillop spoke much about the third degree of obedience, although not in those terms. She frequently urged Sisters not to judge and not to express their opinions, but to give way to the one in authority. Superiors may judge and criticise because, as it were, they are large stars in the constellation, to revert to Ignatius' metaphor, but little stars – 'the poor religious, who forget themselves and constitute themselves judges, where they should be humble and docile subjects'[12] – are doing greater harm to themselves and others than they know. She concludes her letter to the Sisters: 'Believe me I have reason to warn you of this'. What did she mean? She does not elaborate. However, it was only ten days after she had written to Dr Campbell[13] in Rome at length, telling him how misunderstood she had been when she had given her opinion, unasked, to Dr Reynolds,[14] regarding the difficulties she saw in carrying out the decisions of the Apostolic Commission. Did she reflect on what Ignatius had said, that it would have been prudent to keep silent? She must have been so hurt to have her genuine questions treated as being 'in opposition to the views of the Apostolic Commission', which she had never intended. On that occasion, the Commission had failed to recognise the brightness of the star that Mary MacKillop was.

On another occasion she tells the Sisters not to contend, that is, not to strive to be right. That is something that even today we want – to be right, and to have our opinions noted. She wrote:

> Sisters of St Joseph should never love their own opinions … Let us be ready to give way. We are never sure that we are right; and even when we are nearly sure let us not

contend. When we have given our opinion humbly and quietly, let us sacrifice the rest for love of God.[15]

She was markedly influenced by Ignatius in what she said. She knew from her own experience how easy it is for there to be misunderstanding when a Sister tries to explain and justify her actions. Obedience of the understanding is a more dignified way of handling disputes.

Obedience of the understanding is also needed when Religious seek to keep their opinions and feelings in harmony, so that they can obey 'with love and cheerfulness', by keeping their opinions to themselves. However, the understanding does not have the freedom of the will since it is constrained by the truth. But there are many matters of opinion where the understanding with the help of the will can decide one thing is right and another is wrong. For example, a Provincial is convinced that the idea of a 'stolen' generation is mistaken, but he will accept the description of a 'lost' generation. A Religious believes that 'stolen' generation describes accurately what happened but he (or she) listens to the Provincial's judgment and does not rely on their own contrary judgment even if they believe they are right. A brother or sister must think the same as the Provincial as far as this is possible. Ignatius believes that it is expedient to relinquish our will and not attempt to have our own way in the matter, but to conform to the Superior's wisdom so that we do not risk sacrificing our unity.

The hardest example of obedience is what Ignatius calls 'blind obedience'. He refers to God telling Abraham to sacrifice his son, Isaac. This is a case of 'blind obedience'. Abraham does not ask why or demur, or protest. He is not reluctant or defiant. He simply takes his son to the place of sacrifice, obeying blindly. At the last moment he is not required to sacrifice Isaac. What was Abraham's state of mind? He was going to let God have his son, the dearest object in his life, without question, because he has heard the voice of God (*obedire*) and had a consuming desire to desire what God desired.

Obedience, for both Ignatius and Mary MacKillop, involves the total self-transcendent giving to God out of the desire for God. Ignatius spoke of obedience as:

> … a holocaust in which the whole man (or woman) without the slightest reserve is offered in the fire of charity to his Creator and Lord.

This is what the story of Abraham illustrates. Obedience in the Religious life is the wholehearted desire for God, expressed by Merton as the centre of the soul welling up and filling the whole person with an awareness of God.

The centre of the soul wells up with desire for God. This overwhelming desire for God lifts us above petty disagreements. Nothing matters except our oneness in God. As Teilhard de Chardin reminds us, God is only concerned with reality, not with appearances. The tiffs and quarrels that break out in communities are only disturbances on the surface. The reality is our oneness in God. Mary MacKillop wanted all her Sisters to know the source of their unity and how superficial their differences of opinion really were.

The desire for God is no longer what might be called daily obedience in little things; it is a once and for all obedience. It is the obedience a Religious vows to God, to put God first forever.

I have stressed that obedience is a much misunderstood term. It does not mean doing what you are told. Even Ignatius, writing over five centuries ago, said as much. Obedience was important for Mary MacKillop because she followed Ignatius in maintaining that obedience was essential for unity.

Obedience is a much needed virtue in Religious life today, as well as in everyday life. Its root is 'obedire' which means to listen hard for the voice of God. In the world of noise and so many competing voices, we need to listen with all our attention for the still, small voice that will come if all our desire is for God. God's desire is for each of us to have the freedom to choose what God desires.

# 8

## Mary MacKillop and Friendship

*Friendships are not sustained by blood or genes but only by love freely shared. This makes them both more vulnerable and ultimately stronger than any other kind of relationship.*

Sandra Schneiders

There has been an interest in friendship since the fifth century BC, the time of Plato and Aristotle. From Plato, we have derived the saying 'platonic friendship', meaning friendship without sex or erotic behaviour. Aristotle was concerned with the question of who can be friends. Can a citizen and a slave be friends? Friends need to be equal. Plato and Aristotle were interested in friendship because they recognised its human value. At the same time, they did not think that just anybody could be friends. There was the good of society to consider.

When we come to Mary MacKillop it is not the good of society but the good of Religious life that has to be considered. I am going to start by disposing of what some might think is a problem regarding Religious life and friendship. Mary MacKillop had many friends, and it would be true to say that she had one special friend: Joanna Barr Smith. There is something very beautiful about the friendship between these two women, one of whom was a Religious, the other a happily married woman. They are like two opals in the sand, shining in the sun. It is a very privileged and intimate task to look into their friendship, as far as it is possible.

Some people see a problem with friendship for a Religious. It raises questions, such as: How important are our friends to us? How important should they be for a Religious? These questions arise from a fundamental issue, namely, the place of personal relationships and our relationship with God. Nothing can be allowed to come between God and us. Of course, that applies to the laity as well as Religious.

I was interested to discover, when I was reading Shirley du Boulay's biography of Teresa of Avila,[1] and at the same time mulling over the problem of friendship, that Teresa had wrestled with the same problem I had had from my early teens: How could I love God more than I loved my friends? God was bodiless; no face, no smile, no eyes and no arms. I loved my friends dearly, some of them quite passionately. Could I try to love God more? It was a question of the priority of friendship with God over my friendships with human friends. Did I have a choice to make between them and God? I never made that choice consciously, though I pondered the question long and hard.

When Teresa was about forty, she underwent what people have described as a second conversion. From that experience, she knew that friendships would always be important to her but they had ceased to threaten to come between her and God. There was no longer any conflict between human friendships and God for her. God was the centre of her life. Shirley du Boulay writes: 'She would never again be able to sustain an affectionate relationship with anyone whose first concern was not with God and prayer.' The solution for Teresa was to realise that her love for her friends was an expression of her love for God. So, human friendship and friendship with God are compatible. Another way of putting the matter is to acknowledge that a friend is a gift from God, and, like a favourite piece of music, easy to be with, harmonious and sometimes restful, like strings, while at other times full of life, like *timpani*. St Aelred has a more practical approach: he likened a friend to a walking stick, a help when the road gets rough.

There is no evidence that Mary MacKillop was troubled by this dilemma. God was always first in her life, then the Institute and its Rule, and finally, family and friends. She did not seem to see any inconsistency between her particular friendship with Joanna Barr Smith and the Rule of the Institute, which denied the Sisters the right to have particular friendships. Part of what I shall contend is that her friendship with Joanna made her a more delightfully whole human person, without in any way detracting from her holiness. Joanna Barr Smith was the only special friend she had ever had, her childhood was so wrapped up in caring for the family.

Mary and Joanna were certainly equals, though not financially. Joanna was a wealthy woman. Her husband, Robert Barr Smith, was the wealthiest man in South Australia at the time. Mary had known financial hardship all her life. But Mary was a well-educated woman and so was Joanna. Robert had had a university education. Mary's father had been educated for the priesthood in Rome and at Blair College, Aberdeen. He had passed on his knowledge and love of the Church to Mary. They were both very spiritual women and, although Joanna and Robert were Protestants and Mary was a Catholic, they were able to discuss spiritual matters.

One might wonder how Mary would have had time for a friendship, given her responsibilities with the Institute, looking after the Sisters and coping with difficult bishops. Towards the end of Mary's life, Joanna remarked that it had been an unbroken friendship of nearly forty years. Of the forty years, Mary had spent only about seven interrupted years altogether in Adelaide and South Australia, where Joanna had her home. For much of the time, Mary was in Queensland or Sydney, establishing convents. There were few occasions when they could meet. So they corresponded. Joanna was a very frank, and sometimes amusing correspondent.

Mary had a strong bond with Julian Tenison Woods, the co-founder of the Institute, especially at the beginning when they shared the dream of a Sisterhood for the education of poor children living in the bush, and saw it come into being. This would have given them great joy. Consequently, it was a great sadness to her when their relationship deteriorated and, try as she might, there was no mending of it. It was a cross she had to carry.

When looking into Mary MacKillop's friendship with Joanna Barr Smith, I have found William Modystack's book on Mary MacKillop very helpful. He quotes mainly from Joanna's letters and traces the development of their friendship.

Nearly all the evidence that there was a close friendship between Mary and Joanna is from Joanna's letters to Mary. Fayette Gosse[2] has also shed light on the relationship between them. Again, it is from Joanna's letters; but in some cases it is possible to work out how Mary would have responded to these letters. Joanna writes warmly and affectionately and it is obvious that her feelings for Mary run deep, but one senses that it is not just one-sided. Joanna has a great admiration for Mary, whom Fayette Gosse describes as, 'This terrifically inspired and active little nun'. Joanna particularly admired Mary's faith. Fayette Gosse points out that she 'would have liked to have such faith and the comfort deriving from it'. Yet she was unable to accept Catholicism and she was true to herself in the matter.

In what follows I shall look at different questions and endeavour to show that their friendship is a testament to their rich and gifted humanity. The first question is: what kind of friend was Mary? Secondly, what was the attraction between Mary and Joanna? And thirdly, how did their friendship blossom?

## Mary as a Friend

There does not seem to be any record of how Mary and Joanna met. Robert and Joanna Barr Smith arrived in Adelaide from Melbourne in 1856, some ten years before Mary left Penola to come to Adelaide. The Barr Smiths were great workers for charity and it is more than likely that they met, or at least heard of, Mary MacKillop in the course of doing charitable work in the late 1860s. When Mary returned from Queensland in 1871, she heard of the Barr Smith's tragedy in the loss of their third child. She visited them to express her sympathy. Mary knew the sadness of losing a child. When her little brother, Alick, died, she had suffered with her mother, Flora. She knew something of the pain that Joanna had been through. From that time, Joanna and Mary became friends.

In a letter to her mother, written on 21 January 1873, Mary spoke of Joanna:

> They (the Barr Smiths) move in the highest society here, and Mrs R B Smith is an elegant and accomplished Scotch lady. She is a woman of very superior mind, and why she should so singularly attach herself to me I cannot understand. Both she and her husband know that my earnest desire is for her conversion, and I hope for much good from her visit to Rome and other parts of the Continent.[3]

Mary makes it quite clear here that the way of friendship with Joanna is to initiate and foster Catholic faith in Joanna's soul. But friendship is when two people give themselves freely and unconditionally to one another. However, not only was Mary hoping to convert Joanna, but Joanna was hoping for spiritual guidance and help from Mary – something she had not been able to find in anyone else to her satisfaction. So their friendship promised to be mutually enriching.

What kind of friend was Mary MacKillop? There are all kinds of friends – cautious, generous, demanding, jealous, affectionate, over-sensitive, forgiving, understanding, loyal, and so on.

We have just seen that Mary was a sympathetic friend, certainly over the deaths of Joanna's children. Joanna had thirteen children. Six of them died in childhood. It was a prolonged, heartbreaking loss. After the death of another of her children, she wrote to Mary:

> My dear friend, I thank you for your most kind and wonderful letter. I won't say more, but I will read your book – nay, more I will try to pray.[4]

One can imagine the comfort she derived from Mary's letter of sympathy and how Mary would have tried to encourage her to have faith. Unfortunately we do not know what the book was that she sent her. One has the feeling that Joanna's scepticism may have been increased by the loss of so many babies, and her faith in a loving and merciful God shaken. So it says a lot for the effect that Mary had on her when Joanna says 'I will try to pray'.

Joanna valued the comfort of a deeply religious friend but she wanted more than that from their friendship. She was ardently searching for spiritual truth. She wrote to Mary from Brussels on 30 November 1873:

> Ah, if only I could believe in the efficacy of prayer ... But you know my hard, unbelieving spirit. I seem to get worse everyday. I wonder you can take the very faintest interest in me for I must continually wound your spirit and vex your heart.[5]

Circumstances did not look propitious for a deep and lasting friendship between them. Joanna was a Protestant and Mary was a Catholic who would have loved to convert Joanna. In a letter to her mother in 1873, Mary spoke of her hope of converting Joanna. But that was not to be. She wrote to Joanna on 17 October 1873, from Liverpool in Britain:

> Do tell me when you next write how your convictions now stand upon *the one thing necessary*. I cannot believe that your mind is at rest upon this point, and until it is, you know that the true heartfelt affection of my poor self for you will never be satisfied.[6]

I do not know what the one thing necessary was – perhaps the need to pray – but what she says shows how much Joanna's spiritual disease affected her. There would always be an ache in her heart for her dearest friend to become a Catholic and to know the peace and joy of true faith. When Mary wrote to Joanna that 'her heartfelt affection ... will never be satisfied', Joanna may have felt that she was a disappointment to Mary. But she would have felt even more of a disappointment to her beloved husband, Robert, who was also a Protestant, if she were to become a Catholic. She knew he would not change.

As a friend, Mary certainly put God first, but she is deeply concerned for her friend, whom she knows is spiritually unsettled and searching. She had to be a very understanding friend, and she never put pressure on Joanna to accept Catholicism.

Mary was not a cautious friend. Her friendship with Joanna was no doubt a matter for comment from those who were interfering busybodies. She did not appear to mind what people said. Robert, on the other hand, complained to Mary:

> My wife has been the subject of much remark lately in connection with your church & there are now many people who will not believe when told she is not a Catholic.[7]

Fayette Gosse comments that this 'in no way stemmed the friendship' between Mary and Joanna, who continued to meet when they were in Adelaide and to correspond when they could not meet. Joanna, like Mary, it seems, was not a cautious person, when it came to avoiding tittle-tattle for gossips.

From the beginning, they had much in common. They were both deeply concerned for the underprivileged. Joanna was keenly interested in Mary's plans – for education for those who could not afford it and for the women's Refuge and the Providence that Mary and Julian Tenison Woods set up in Adelaide. They were both very generous people. Joanna was wealthy and gave liberally, as did her husband. She and Robert helped Mary financially many times. Mary also loved to give to anyone in need. She could not give large sums of money but she was known to give her dinner to a vagrant and go hungry herself.

Friendships do not always run smoothly. There was one occasion when Joanna hurt Mary by not coming to a reception at a new convent and not sending any reply to her invitation. She wrote to Mary on 16 January 1873, saying:

> I was very glad to receive your kind note. I do not know in what way I can have given you to understand that I was no longer your friend except by not sending any reply to your last note.[8]

Obviously, Mary had felt that there was a lack of friendship on Joanna's part. She had not come and she had not written, not even a brief note of acknowledgment. Her reasons for not replying were a little uncharitable. When she did eventually write to Mary she explained that, at the time, 'there were a great many disagreeable things said about the Sisterhood as a body. Although my sympathies were always with you and several others ...they were not with all.' Joanna allowed herself to be influenced by what people were saying about the Sisters. She finished her letter by saying that she had had many months of ill-health and was not recovering well from her last pregnancy, and complains that Mary made no effort to write to her.

Their friendship had its ups and downs, like life itself, which shows that it was real. There was genuine emotion involved at this stage: disappointment on Mary's side that Joanna had not come, and self-pity and a little shame on Joanna's. It was a case for forgiveness on Mary's part and that would always be forthcoming. She was a most forgiving person.

Mary and Joanna were abroad at the same time in 1873. Joanna left Adelaide with her family on 31 January. Mary left for Rome in March of the same year. They had planned to meet in Rome but that did not eventuate. That must have been a disappointment to Mary, who had hopes that Rome would help to bring about a conversion in Joanna. After Rome, Mary went to London, and there she met Joanna who was returning from Scotland to Brussels. Mary wrote to her sister, Annie:

> Mrs R Barr Smith (that kind Adelaide friend of whom I have sometimes spoken in letters to Mamma) is coming from Scotland to stay a few months in London. She has written to tell me so and we are mutually looking forward to a happy meeting for there is much feeling in common between us.[9]

Those few words speak volumes about their friendship. It was a close friendship and they were both rejoicing in a happy prospect of meeting and spending time together. Mary may have been feeling a little lonely in the vast city of London, and missing her Sisters, but the mutuality she speaks of leaves us in no doubt that there was a bond of genuine affection between them. There is so much she wishes to share with her friend, and so much she wishes to know about her friend's spiritual state.

Mary demanded a lot of herself as a friend. She knew what she wanted to say to Joanna that she felt would bring her peace of mind. However, sometimes she lost her own peace of mind, as she considered how she should say something and whether she should say it at all. We can see this from the following episode, that happened when Joanna was leaving London to return to her family in Brussels. Writing to her from Liverpool on 17 October, Mary said:

> My dearest friend, I have pondered much whether I should ask you this, and have even now a little note in my bag which I wrote on the night of the day I last saw you, and in which I begged of you to let me see you for a few minutes before you started for the Continent. But I failed in my resolution of sending you this, and ever since I feel myself reproached as if in this I did not do what our good God wanted me to do.[10]

There was something Mary wished to ask Joanna. Unfortunately we don't know what – something she had left unsaid, and must have decided it was important enough to go and see her before Joanna left London. She wrote a little note begging her to let her see her just for a few minutes, put it in her bag, and proceeded to worry about whether she should send it or not, with the result that she did nothing about it. And then she wrote to Joanna telling her everything, quite frankly, and saying that she felt reproached for not doing what she was sure God wanted her to do, namely, send the note. This shows how human Mary was and how much her relations with Joanna mattered to her. We all know the uncertainty of whether or not we should do something, particularly when it involves someone we care about. This is surely a testament to their very human friendship.

## What was the Attraction Between Them?

Joanna seems to have been attracted to Mary from the beginning. We know this from a letter she wrote to Mary in 1871, in which she said:

You have always had a wonderful attraction for me, and however undeserving I am, I hope you won't withdraw your friendship from me entirely … I have often found myself thinking of you as of something serene and peaceful far, far removed from me … I wear your locket and shall wear it for ever for your sake – so that I can always feel I have loved a good woman – who has tried to do me some good.[11]

The 'wonderful attraction' Mary had for her was her faith. Joanna speaks longingly of the serene peacefulness of Mary MacKillop because she herself was not peaceful. She had what she called a questioning, sceptical spirit, which made her at times very unhappy, and which she said she was unable to change. When she speaks of the possibility that Mary would stop being her friend, she is thinking of Mary's commitment to Catholicism and her own shaky Protestant belief. There was this gulf at the heart of their friendship, which Joanna felt keenly when she wrote this letter. Mary longed for her friend to receive the gift of faith and have the opportunity to become a Catholic. It never happened, but it never affected their relationship. There was a bond of affection between them. The locket must have been a keepsake that Mary had given Joanna. What a very human thing to do; a simple expression of love, that Mary knew would mean such a lot to Joanna. It was as though Mary was the person Joanna would dearly have loved to be herself – serene and peaceful. To have her as a friend was the next best thing.

There were many things that reminded Joanna of Mary. She wrote from Brussels to Mary and commented on St Gudule, the beautiful old cathedral, which was close by where they lived in Brussels. She said, 'I always think of you whenever I look at it or hear the deep, solemn chimes'. Mary's deep voice attracted her and the cathedral's booming chimes brought Mary's voice to mind, and she loved to listen to them.

What was it about Joanna that attracted Mary? Joanna probably had a Scottish voice or intonation that would have appealed to

Mary. She might well have been softly spoken, as many Scottish women are, which could explain why Fayette Gosse remarks that Mary often spoke of Joanna as 'gentle Joanna'. But she may also have had a gentle disposition. Mary must have relished and respected her 'superior mind'. They could discuss on an equal footing. Mary must have loved Joanna's care for her large family and love for her husband. But what attracted Mary more than anything else was Joanna's passionate searching for spiritual faith. Mary knew that she needed a spiritual friend and it was a dictum of the Institute to 'Never see a need without trying to meet it'. Mary did try, and it was not easy. Joanna wrote to her in 1899:

> I get very down on my luck sometimes and in fact there does not seem anything now to live for. You will say this is a very unhealthy and unholy attitude of mind. I grant this, darling Mother, but there's something fundamentally wrong with me – in mind and heart.[12]

This may have been depression; but if she had opened her mind and heart to the Catholic faith, I feel this is not the way she would have written to Mary.

As with all friendships, there was a mystery about the friendship between Joanna and Mary. Mary herself, as we have seen, writes to her mother that she cannot understand why Joanna Barr Smith should have attached herself to her in such a singular way. There is no mystery for Joanna, who had never known such a courageous person, so committed to the Will of God and to the education of poor children. She was certainly attracted to Mary.

## How did their Friendship Blossom?

At the beginning of their friendship, they were able to meet in Adelaide and then in London. These meetings enabled them to lay the foundations of their friendship by talking freely about spiritual matters – about the Catholic faith and the efficacy of prayer. Mary also raised with Joanna the importance of unity for the Institute and other matters. From Modystack, we learn that Joanna was aware of the problems Mary had with the Institute.

At the same time, Joanna needed a sympathetic friend who could help her with the deaths of her children and the effect these deaths had upon her belief in a merciful God. It was the need for sympathy that drew Mary to her in the beginning.

Early on in their friendship, Joanna and Robert were benefactors of the Institute. The Sisters had purchased properties from them, no doubt at favourable prices. In 1872, when the Sisters took possession of the Kensington property in Adelaide which was their Mother house, Robert and Joanna donated money for it; and also gave two paintings for the chapel (which are still there today). Throughout the forty years of their friendship with Mary, Joanna and Robert were very liberal. The fact that they were very wealthy did not impinge on the friendship of the two women, which in itself is a wonderful testament to their affection and trust.

When Mary became settled in Sydney in 1883, there were not the same opportunities for them to meet. For twenty-six years, they lived in two different worlds, but they kept in touch by letter.

In 1902, Mary suffered a stroke in Auckland, New Zealand. When Joanna heard of Mary's illness, she wrote to Mary:

> Ah, my dear, darling Mother and friend, I realised how much you were to me when the fear arose that I was going to lose you. The past rose up before me – the faraway years where you and I first became friends – my cravings to find rest and peace in your communion and all the affection and sympathy I received. Although latterly we have drifted apart, my old love for you remains unaltered. Distance can make no difference.[13]

What a heartfelt tribute to her old friend. I see this as evidence of the blossoming of their friendship. There is no rushing to see each other before one or other of them departs for some other part of the world. Joanna has learnt what we all have to learn – that distance makes no difference. She looks back on the past with gratitude. She may have been thinking of Mary's saying, 'Gratitude is the memory of the heart'. I see the influence of Mary MacKillop in the loving way Joanna expresses herself. There is no spiritual craving now. She surely has attained the peace and serenity that she craved so badly in the beginning. Knowing all the hardships Mary had had in her life and her complete trust in God, must have had some effect on Joanna Barr Smith. In 1907, Mary wrote an 'Appeal of the Sacred Heart to a weary disappointed soul'. She sent a copy to Joanna, who wrote back:

> Ah dearest Mother Mary, we are all weary and disappointed when we get old. Well for us if we have some hope of life beyond this. I like your little paper so much. It speaks to my heart.[14]

Mary's paper is an expression of her love for the Sacred Heart. If it speaks to Joanna's heart, her heart must have been filled with sentiment that could only be called Catholic. She must have leant out of her Protestant stance and set her heart free to love the Sacred Heart. There is none of the scepticism, doubting, and questioning that used to trouble her. In the same letter, she writes:

> Oh, my dear friend, I wish I could see you again, or hear your voice ... Living or dying – my beloved friend – I am ever the same to you.[15]

Joanna's final token to their unbroken friendship of nearly forty years was the very beautiful marble tomb that is in the Chapel at Mount Street. Joanna's words bring tears to my eyes: 'Living or dying ... I am ever the same to you'. She was as generous in death as she had been in life. Was it her love for Mary or Mary's love for her which had prompted her generosity? There is no answer to that question because the question itself is the hallmark of genuine friendship that had blossomed in such a natural, human way.

I started with a dilemma, namely: what is the place of human friendships in relation to friendship with God? I pointed out that this did not seem to have been a dilemma for Mary. God had always come first in her life. I have tried to show that her friendship with Joanna made her more of a whole, rounded, human person.

# 9

## *The Wisdom of Mary MacKillop*

*The most conspicuous thing about her was that she was a Catholic nun; however, she conveyed the Christian Faith to those around her, not by exhortation, or discourse, or by polemic, but in herself. What they saw in her was a living faith, expressed in personal love.*

Positio

The testimony of Mary MacKillop's Sisters and friends regarding her virtues was unanimous. As Paul Gardiner writes in the *Positio*:

> It was agreed everywhere that she was very nice. That is hardly a subtle theological analysis, but it is a good rough-and-ready reaction to somebody whose heart was full of genuine charity ... The impression left by the evidence is that of her niceness, her kindness, her concern for all, her goodness.[1]

From this, it seems that she was not especially known for her wisdom. It was particularly her kindness that people who knew her remembered her for. The philosopher, Wittgenstein, once said that what the world needed most was kindness. Nowadays, in the rush of daily life, with the confusion of world economics and talk of global recession, which affects us all, the world needs wisdom more than ever, particularly the wisdom of reconciliation

As well as a 'heart full of genuine charity', Mary MacKillop certainly was a wise woman, but did she have wisdom? We use the word 'wise' rather loosely to mean prudent, level-headed, discreet or circumspect, even clever. What do we mean when we talk about wisdom? We might mean all or none of these things, because wisdom has a theological meaning as well as an ethical one, and it is that I want to flesh out to begin with in relation to Mary MacKillop.

I shall start by examining further what is meant by wisdom and seeing how far Mary MacKillop can be said to have had wisdom. I shall go on to give some examples of what I believe is her wisdom.

## The Theological Meaning of Wisdom

There has been a tendency in theology to associate wisdom with mysticism; that is to say, with experience that has a divine or sacred significance, surpassing ordinary understanding. Wisdom is not a matter for the intelligence or intellect. It is much more a matter of the heart and insight.

A word that is frequently used to describe wisdom is 'radiance':

> Wisdom is radiant and unfading and she is easily discerned by those who love her. (Wisd. 6:12)

This suggests that something is revealed but not necessarily understood, and to be lived with in one's heart.

Wisdom is also spoken of as leading to 'friendship with God':

> God loves nothing so much as the person who lives with wisdom. (Wisd. 7:14 and 28)

Andrew Louth, in his introduction to *The Wisdom of the Greek Fathers,* gives an example of what would generally be thought of as wisdom. He writes:

> God ... as the source of our being is closer to us than we are ourselves.[2]

That may seem mystifying at first. God is in the depths of our being, a part of ourselves that we are often shy about visiting. Therefore we are able to say that God is closer to us than we are ourselves. He knows the hidden depths of our being that are not so well known to us. Mary MacKillop says something similar in a letter to her Sisters:

> God understands us better than we understand ourselves or each other.[3]

This is a truth that she is afraid her Sisters have not grasped or at least that they have not acted on, as she would have wished. She is not saying anything as paradoxical as 'God is closer to us than we are to ourselves', but she is pointing out that, because God understands each one far better than they understand themselves, they must allow God room to deal with each one in his own way and not interfere. She goes on to say in the same letter that God wants us to 'lean more on Him and less on ourselves'. There is wisdom in what she says, for we want to be in control of our lives and we do not give God enough space to come closer in friendship, lest we lose some of our control.

The meaning of wisdom that many mystics give us is that of seeking the closeness or oneness between God and ourselves. Another way of putting it is that, in order to find God, we must first find ourselves. As St Teresa of Avila puts it, 'we shall never succeed in knowing ourselves unless we seek to know God'.[4] The aim and object of finding ourselves and finding God is union between God and the self. The German mystic, Meister Eckhart puts it:

> The love that someone gives contains not two but one and oneness and when I love I am more God than I am in myself.[5]

When someone loves, it is an experience of two becoming one, and of being spiritually enlarged by the oneness so that the experience is of becoming one with God. There is a sense of the wonder of union. Thomas a Kempis writes:

> Then all that is within me shall rejoice exceedingly, when my soul shall be perfectly united to God ... This is my whole desire that my heart be united to you.[6]

Mary MacKillop came close to expressing the same ecstasy when she wrote:

> ... we become alive only to the longing desires of our Spouse (Christ) for the perfection of our souls, performing

all our actions, joining in the crowd or shrinking from it, receiving the blind praise of creatures or their severest criticism – All alike – all in God and for God.[7]

She is speaking of a total immersion in God. Nothing matters to her except that we should desire the perfection that Christ longs for each to have. All are in God, at one with God; and all are for God, united in joy. There is a certain mysticism about what she says, in the sense that she takes us beyond ordinary understanding, as the writer of the Wisdom of Solomon does when he speaks of wisdom as 'a breath of the power of God' (Wisd. 7:25).

The writer of the book of Sirach tells us that, 'To fear the Lord is the beginning of wisdom' (Sir. 1:14). Mary MacKillop knew what it was to fear the Lord. Her fear was not fear in the sense of being afraid but rather of reverence, awe and wonder at the goodness and kindness of God. She wrote to her mother:

> In the trials, annoyances and anxieties we daily experience, Oh! May we ever recognise that loving Fatherly hand that only seeks to draw us closer to Himself by giving us opportunities of suffering something with him.

She speaks about God drawing us closer to himself. She had no inhibitions or 'hang-ups' about God who wants to be close to us. It is the search for the closeness between God and ourselves that is the core meaning of wisdom.

She undoubtedly was close to God. Father Clune has said he felt that 'Her union with God was continuous. Her life one prayer'.[8] She longed for her Sisters to be as close to God as she was herself. She believed that the Rule would lead them into union with God. She wrote:

> Study it (the Rule) well … Ponder it carefully. See how it tries to lead you to the closest, most intimate union with the will of your God.[9]

## The Language of Mystics

There are many strands of mystical wisdom in the writings of
Mary MacKillop. Mystics have a facility with language that in itself
is quite awe-inspiring. The language of paradox characterises all
forms of mysticism. It is not a rational or intellectual linguistic
ability. It is more poetic – 'Love is not consolation, it is light'
(Simone Weil) – and it is direct in its brevity. Because of their
insights, mystics need an inspired, creative use of language which
seems to come, as a gift, from God himself, or else from deep
within them:

> I prayed and understanding was given me; I called on God
> and the spirit of wisdom came to me. (Wisd. 7:7 and 8)

The spirit of wisdom is not an ability that we can strive for. It is
something that is given to us from God or comes to us from
beyond ourselves and is certainly beyond our control. Mystics
invite us to contemplate what we sense are deep truths:

> God is infinite in his simplicity and simple in his infinity.[10]

We need to spend time with this, dwelling on its meaning. God is
both infinitely great and yet utterly simple. God is both creator of
the heavens and a butterfly's wing. There is often something
abstract about the mystics' wisdom whereas Mary's is more con-
crete, as this example shows:

> We are here in religion, and the work we have to do is to
> let the Will of God be accomplished in us by our becoming
> saints.[11]

Most of Mary MacKillop's writing was in the form of letters to her
Sisters, who did not have a great deal of time to spend in
contemplation or mystical wonderment. They were mostly fully
occupied with teaching duties and Mary's letters were full of wise
encouragement to them. We could hardly expect her to write to
them in the same vein as Meister Eckhart. But she does ardently
encourage them to pray:

... go often in spirit to the Sacred Heart of Jesus and there pour out your supplications for what you desire. You know the kind of visit I mean – one of lively faith, clinging confidence.[12]

Mary is trying to promote closeness and unity between Jesus and each of the Sisters. She is really urging them to become one with Jesus through their prayers to him. In this way she believes peace, unity and charity will be achieved in their life together.

## The Ethical Meaning of Wisdom

Robert Wicks offers a definition of wisdom as 'ordinariness combined with sound practical knowledge'. Wisdom in this sense is much more human and concerned with living life. Mary was known for her practical common sense. There is a beauty and simplicity in ordinariness. Mary MacKillop had no airs and graces. As we say today: 'What you see is what you get.' This may seem to capture very well the meaning of wisdom for Mary MacKillop. But I feel that she has more than practical knowledge and ordinariness to draw on for her wisdom. She has a large, compassionate heart.

It is not hard to find examples of Mary MacKillop's wisdom. My own sense is that her wisdom leads us to think mainly of her gifts of gratitude, reconciliation and a sense of justice. But like so many writers, biblical and others, she knew the wisdom of seeking and doing the Will of God.

## The Wisdom of God's Will

Wisdom comes from God and is responsible for our response to doing his will. This is how Meister Eckhart, puts the matter:

Where God finds his own will, he gives himself and enters in with all that he is. And the more we cease to be in our own will, the more truly we begin to be in God's Will.[13]

Mary knew how to exchange her will for the Will of God so as to be able to co-operate with God. God's Will was the dearest, most precious thing in her life. She knew the wisdom of ceasing to want her own will and only wanting the Will of God. She tended to use the language of affection when speaking of the Will of God: 'To me the Will of God is a dear book.' In other places she speaks of the 'adorable' Will of God and of his 'beautiful' will. In her letter to Monsignor Kirby, she says that she had 'the greatest desire to be able to do God's Will in the most perfect way at any cost'.[14] There is an ardour about how she puts the matter. It is as though doing God's Will in the most perfect way was what her heart longed for. 'Fulfilling his will was her total preoccupation; loving him filled her heart.'[15] There is a closeness between her and God that is tantamount to loving his will. Jesus also loved the Will of God, and said: 'My food is to do the will of him who sent me and to complete his work' (John 4:34). Her passion for the Will of God and the Cross show that her heart is very much involved in her wisdom.

## The Wisdom of Gratitude

The psalmist writes 'Teach me wisdom in the depths of my heart' (Ps. 51), or, as Nan Merrill translates it, 'Teach me the wisdom of the heart'.[16] In the depths of Mary's heart, there was the wisdom of gratitude. As Paul Gardiner writes:

> Whenever she looked about her she was grateful. To God first of all and above all, but then to all those who had been his ministers in bringing her the good things she enjoyed. She never ceased to thank her mother for the early training in the Faith, which meant so much to her. And she was very conscious of how much she owed to her father.[17]

Mary saw so much to be grateful to God for. Gratitude was the natural expression of her heart. So was humility. Mary, like so many wise people, knew the value of humility. Gratitude and humility go together. Humility is forgetfulness of self. In gratitude one leaves oneself behind in being thankful to the other. Thankfulness to God for God's generous bounty brought her close to the God who loved her.

She was always grateful to those who helped her, especially on her travels, from the Marchioness of Lothian, who offered her hospitality, to the young men who had gone with her to the station in Rome. Her gratitude was to the greatest and the least equally.

One of the loveliest sayings of Mary MacKillop that is frequently quoted is: 'Gratitude is the memory of the heart'.[18] There is great wisdom in that. To be thankful for what one remembers, especially what is in the heart, what people have done for you, is to spread a mantle of joy over the past that sheds a brightness on the present as well. Memory is like handing everything over to God held in the palms of one's hands, and saying thank you.

Robert Wicks believes that gratitude can give a whole new perspective in life. He writes:

> Deep gratitude opens us up so we can have a new sense of perspective, no matter what happens in life.[19]

A perspective is a way of looking at something. The new perspective that gratitude brings is to be thankful to God for whatever happens, as Mary always was. This opens the gateway to wisdom. It is a wisdom that we all need to have. Deep gratitude comes from the heart and it is when we are faced with tough realities in life, as she constantly was, that a new perspective enabled her to give thanks and to regard whatever it was as gift rather than disaster. There is always something to be learned from gratitude. 'It is right to give God thanks,' even for the smallest things: a note from a friend, a change of air. Mary, in her wisdom, always gave thanks for everything.

One day we were having a birthday dinner party and it was my job to set the table. I had done everything except a flower for the table. The garden looked bare. I went hopefully to the camellia bushes but they had no flowers. I wandered around the garden but I could find nothing. In my frustration, I murmured: 'Surely, God, there must be just one flower somewhere. All I need is just one little flower. It's not asking for much.' I rounded the corner of the house and saw, lifting up its head from the bare ground, a single yellow freesia, quite perfect, with sprays of buds on either side of open flowers. I thanked God with all the gratitude of my heart. It was such a little thing but it spoke to me of the heart of God who wanted to surprise and delight me.

To be grateful, a person has to take her eyes off herself and forget about herself in order to appreciate another. This attitude is so much needed today, when people are self-centred and caught up in the pursuit of self-interest. We can pray that Mary will teach us the wise way of humility and gratitude.

## The Wisdom of Reconciliation

Reconciliation is closely associated with gratitude. It is when we are conscious of thankfulness in our own hearts that we can forgive whoever has wronged us. How can we persist in hostility towards anyone when our hearts are overflowing in gratitude, as Mary's was? She knew that she needed to forgive priests, bishops and even her own Sisters. She followed her heart in being ready to forgive, especially at the time of her own troubles, her unjust excommunication. She wrote to Father Woods:

> … our poor dear Sisters feel that they are in the hands of bitter enemies instead of those of loved pastors. The poor dear gentlemen, from my heart I forgive them everything, but grieve to think that I have seen what I have seen or heard what I have heard.[20]

These 'poor dear gentlemen' had blamed her, told lies about her and spread rumours about her. Yet she 'forgave them everything'. She will not hold it against them. She is unbelievably forbearing. But it is the wisdom of the heart that enables her to forgive. She knew how sacred relationships are because of the sanctity of her relationship with the Sacred Heart of Jesus, and the responsibility of mending relationships when they are broken.

To the Sisters of South Australia, also at the time of the excommunication, Mary wrote the following, from a letter on forgiveness:

> ... I excuse and with all a mother's heart, I forgive. And as I freely forgive and wish to forget, so do I entreat you, my dearly loved ones to forgive from your hearts any Sister who has pained you, or who you think has wronged you. I want this letter to bring peace to all your hearts.[21]

Some of her own Sisters had spread rumours about her and had not stood by her as they should. She wished there to be a tide of forgiveness sweeping through the minds and hearts of the Sisters, starting with her own 'mother's' heart. She excused and forgave them. That is to say, she made allowances for them. But she knew she had to go further than that. And then, as though she cannot help herself, she forgives them freely, generously, with all her heart and pleads with them all to forgive one another. It shows how much reconciliation meant to her. It is the wisdom of being at peace with one another and flushing out all that would disturb the peace.

Holy Thursday is a special day of reconciliation for the Sisters of St Joseph of the Sacred Heart. There is a tradition in the Congregation to seek forgiveness from one another, particularly on that day. It was a tradition started by Mary that has carried on to today. She wrote to the Sisters in South Australia:

> I ask you to forgive me and pray for me. Forgive all I have done to pain or disedify any one of you ... I feel quite sure ... everyone will be in perfect peace with her Sister – forgiving every little annoyance or slight she may have received from anyone, and freely asking pardon in her turn.[22]

She knew the value of forgiveness and the wisdom of letting go of the niggling pain caused by another, perhaps even inadvertently. It is a cleansing experience, like Jesus washing the feet of the disciples in John's Gospel. It is a joyful experience to be rid of rough edges in relationships, to beg one another's pardon. It is the wisdom of being human.

It seems hard to believe that Mary MacKillop had enemies. She knew there were those who were not well disposed towards her. Speaking of her enemies, she refers to them as her 'loved enemies'. Bishop Cuskelly, writing about Mary's way of love and forgiveness says:

> Of all those whose writings I have read, she is the only one who has written, 'I have through God's wise permission, at present enemies but they are loved enemies'.[23]

She has a deep, wise understanding of reconciliation. It is an attitude of wanting relationships to be mended, of not being prepared to carry a hurt or a grievance lest it should spoil gratitude. Jesus told us to 'Love your enemies'. Mary MacKillop was someone who lived for love. How beautifully and heroically evangelical this attitude really is. If we ponder it, it becomes irresistible wisdom that the world needs so badly at this time. Bishop Cuskelly goes on to say that Mary MacKillop 'could well be the *saint of reconciliation* for all the world'.

## The Wisdom of Justice

Justice, being fair-minded or treating everyone equally often calls for wisdom. Equality mattered a great deal to Mary MacKillop. To her, all people were equal before God. She knew that God had no favourites. Mary was impartial. In her schools, every child, regard-less of wealth or social position, was treated equally. She refused admittance to the Hall School in Adelaide for the Governor's grandson, because his mother wanted special treatment for him. As far as Mary was concerned, everyone was special or nobody was. She knew she could not have a child who was expecting to have privileges, which would have put him in a class of his own. Mary was wise enough not to compromise or break her principles.

When Mary and the Sisters were in Brisbane, a situation developed with the Mercy Sisters. As we know that might have left them feeling very vulnerable and that they had been unjustly treated by the Josephites and parents who preferred the Sisters of St Joseph's more down to earth approach. Mary did the fair-minded thing. She visited the families whose children had left the Mercy schools, to persuade them to send their children back. It did not matter to her that numbers in her own schools would fall as a result. She did not want to be seen as 'poaching' pupils from the Mercies, which was not what had been happening. She could see that it was a matter of justice. How many others finding themselves in such a situation would be wise enough to go to the time-consuming lengths that Mary went to, of visiting each family, for the sake of justice? As a result, there was no ill feeling between the Josephites and the Mercies.

Justice is also concerned with dignity. All people are deserving of honour, all things being equal. Mary was deeply compassionate. She loved the poor, especially poor children. In a letter Sister Lucy wrote to Mother Laurence O'Brien, she told of Mary's arrival at school one day in a snow storm:

> There was a poor little bare-footed and ragged boy stand-ing in class. Mother went straight to him, and putting her arms around him she kissed him saying, 'Ah Sister, these are the children I love'.[24]

One could say that Mary had singled out this little boy for favoured treatment which would not have been exactly just. Yet he must have stood out for her beside his class mates as the most shabbily dressed. She wanted to help him to feel equal and to be able to respect himself. Honour was due to the least as well as to the greatest. Today, when we hear so much about the abuse of children, it is refreshing to remember that a child mattered so much to a saint.

Justice has to do with punishment. How did Mary administer punishment? Being fair was necessary. One time when Mary was visiting Kincumber, there was a knock on her door. 'Come in,' she said, and a small boy walked in and stood before her. She could tell by looking at him that he was in trouble. He confessed to her that he had stolen a bun from the bakery, whereupon Mary asked him if he was hungry. He replied that he was. 'Well go and ask Sister to give you two buns!' This is being just with compassion. Whoever the boy had been, he would have received the same treatment, provided he knew he was in trouble. So often, in reading of Jesus' replies to people, I am amazed at his wisdom, but Mary MacKillop's wisdom in her reply to the boy is similarly breathtaking. It shows her understanding of the boy's plight, her sense of his dignity, and her humanity. There is a story of the Desert Father, Abba Poemen, that brings out the same wisdom:

> A few of the brothers came to see Abba Poemen. They said to him, 'Tell us what to do when we see brothers dozing during prayer. Should we pinch them to help them stay awake?' The elder said to them, 'Actually what I would do if I saw a brother sleeping is to put his head on my knees and let him rest.'[25]

There is the same humane sense of need in the two cases, the boy who was hungry and needed food and the Brother who needed sleep. Humanity and need come before justice and punishment for Mary MacKillop, as they did for Jesus. Being attentive to the needs of others is a Gospel value full of wisdom and compassion.

At the beginning of this chapter, I pointed out two meanings of wisdom. First, the theological meaning, wisdom in the sense of union or friendship with God. Second, the ethical meaning, wisdom in the sense of ordinariness and practical common sense. I believe Mary MacKillop had wisdom in both senses. Father Clune has said, so perceptively: 'Her union with God was continuous. Her life one prayer.' Gratitude, reconciliation and justice were the fruit of her union with God and her life of prayer.

Mary had great wisdom in knowing what people needed. She knew that her Sisters needed to be close to God in friendship and to the Sacred Heart of Jesus. They needed to be able to live with one another in unity, peace and charity. She knew that the little fellow at Kincumber needed food, not scolding. She knew how to forgive people from her heart. Her wisdom is every bit as enlightening as the mystics'. There is much we can learn from it for life today. In particular, her great sense of the need for forgiveness and her willingness to forgive and to ask for forgiveness for herself. As we think about her wisdom, let us acknowledge that it is the wisdom of her practical humanity and her friendship with God that is the gift she has left with us.

# 10
## The Spirituality of Courage –
## Mary MacKillop and
## Helen Prejean

*New life begins when we have the courage to overcome our own
fear and apathy and seek genuine communion with those in
poverty, in pain or in deep need.*

Edwards

There are different kinds of courage. There is the courage that is
gritting one's teeth and stealing oneself to face a disaster. There is
the courage that calls for a quiet commitment to seeing something
through. The spirituality of courage is when one is conscious of
God being with one and lifting one up to meet whatever is
coming. Spiritual courage enables one to say 'I am not alone'.
Mary MacKillop had a deep spring of courage within her. She
never counted the cost, and always faced the obstacle or hardship
calmly, trusting in God.

The name of Sister Helen Prejean CSJ (Congregation
of St Joseph) came to be internationally known when her book
*Dead Man Walking*[1] was first published in 1993. It is described as *An
Eyewitness Account of the Death Penalty* in the United States. Helen
Prejean's mission is the eradication of the death penalty; that calls
for tough courage. I shall endeavour to interweave her challenging
story with that of Mary MacKillop's selfless story.

What is the connection between Mary MacKillop and Helen
Prejean? They are both outstandingly courageous women in the
way they have stood up against opposition. Sadly, most of the
opposition that Mary MacKillop endured came, most unjustly,
from bishops and priests, but she stood her ground, although she
always forgave with great compassion. Helen Prejean faces an
obstacle of quite a different kind, a widespread attitude of hostility

among the American public to any interference with the death penalty. Helen Prejean is a nun, as Mary MacKillop was. She is an American Sister of St Joseph of Medaille, Louisiana. Mary MacKillop is known first and foremost as an educator. She was possibly one of the greatest educators Australia has ever had. Helen Prejean is someone who wants to change the law regarding capital punishment in America – a social reformer.

Helen Prejean's story is very different to Mary MacKillop's. As a child, young woman, and professed nun, she lived comfortably. Her father was a lawyer and her family was well off. She travelled quite extensively in America, Canada and Europe. In 1980, her religious community, the Sisters of St Joseph of Medaille, made a decision to stand with the poor. Helen had hesitatingly agreed. She did not want to grapple with economics and politics. She defended her position by pointing out that Jesus had said 'The poor you will always have with you.' One day, Sister Marie Augusta Neal SND (Sisters of Notre Dame), a sociologist, came to speak about the poor. Helen went to hear her but did not believe she had anything to learn. She prayed for the poor and gave money to the poor. What more could she do? She received a message from Sister Maria Augusta that changed her life: Jesus Christ came to give good news to the poor. The good news was that they would no longer be poor. It was a personal call to her to do something for the poor and marginalised that would actually bring her to meet the poor and eventually to be with the poor. Later, she was asked to write to someone on Death Row, and so she became involved with Matthew Poncelet, of whom she said: 'He is worse than any single person I've ever encountered.' But he needed a friend, and the love of Christ that she could bring him. She wrote:

> When I started out as a young Catholic nun, I had no idea that I would walk this path into America's death chambers. My Catholic faith has been the catalyst to inspire me to follow the way of Jesus who sided with the poor and dispossessed and despised.[2]

Going into death chambers needs more than her own strength. She goes with the consciousness of the presence of Christ with her.

When I was in Adelaide in 2005, I noticed a plaque set in the pavement: 'Mary MacKillop – Social Reformer, 1842–1909'. It puzzled me, because as far as I was aware Mary MacKillop was an educator, not a social reformer. However, it was Adelaide where the Sisters were first established and where they found many destitute poor. She worked with the poor and visited those in prison from the very beginning of the Institute in Adelaide in 1867. New South Wales tends to overlook that fact where her reputation is firmly grounded in education. Was she, like Helen Prejean, a social reformer?

Mary MacKillop visited gaols. And so did Helen Prejean. Both befriended murderers. It is their commitment to those who were facing death as a punishment for the life, or lives, they had taken, sometimes most brutally, that is the connection between them and that I should like to draw attention to. But it must be pointed out that Mary MacKillop's contact with murderers was in the wider context of visiting hospitals, sick rooms and gaols, and sheltering the homeless. Helen Prejean has a mission to the inmates on Death Row – all of whom were awaiting either an unlikely reprieve or a cruel death – '*a thing* waiting to be handled by the executioners,'[3] was how they were thought of. That is an important difference between them, in the sense that Helen was motivated by the terrible human tragedies she had experienced for herself. Mary MacKillop considered the education of poor children to be her main work, but the plight of the poor, the destitute, and criminals, including murderers, was always with her. Why did she become known as a social reformer in South Australia, in spite of the fact that she founded schools in and around Adelaide and had no interest in changing the law?

First of all, I shall consider whether Mary MacKillop is primarily an educator or a social reformer. Secondly, I am going to look at Mary's mission to prisoners. In the third place, I shall say more about the bond between Mary and Helen. And lastly, I shall highlight what I consider to be their outstanding compassion and courage. Frequently, compassion requires courage in order for a person to enter a situation that is full of opposition and even danger.

## Mary MacKillop, Educator or Social Reformer?

When the Institute was founded in 1866, it was brought into being for the education of poor children. There is no doubt that Mary was a gifted and well-prepared teacher who used her gifts for education and to teach children their Catholic faith. She was not only well-prepared herself but made sure her teachers had the necessary text books to be able to give good lessons.

When Mary came to Adelaide in 1867 with Rose Cunningham, they were to take charge of the St Francis Xavier Cathedral Hall School. Before the year was over, two more schools had opened – one at Yankalilla about 75 km from Adelaide, and the other at Brompton, a working class suburb of Adelaide. Seven more schools opened in the second year (1868). Schools staffed by the Sisters of St Joseph were spreading like wild fire. By the end of that year, there were fifty women who had joined Mary; not all professed Sisters and not all trained teachers, but many of them could teach. Father Woods, who was diocesan Director of Education and Inspector of Schools, wrote a favourable report of the schools at the end of 1868, when there were ten schools. There was a desperate need for schools. 'Sisters of St Joseph as educators' would have been a front page story in any local paper. Anything about visiting the gaol or providing refuge for destitute women would only have rated a small paragraph on an inside page.

These schools, however, were for poor children. Mary wrote, in *Aims and Objects:*

> … the great work of the Sisters being the education in a strictly Catholic manner of the children of the poorer class, it becomes necessary for those interested in such a work to understand the general position of persons of this class.[4]

It is a moot point whether she was speaking here as a Catholic educator or as someone with a social conscience, who cared deeply about social reform. If her Sisters were going to teach poor children they had to be prepared to share the poverty of the poor. They were to be known as a mendicant Institute. This, however, has nothing to do with education but with the Josephite under-standing of poverty which might well have led them to urge for reform, except that they were too immersed in their mission to find time to campaign to petition the Government. Becoming involved in politics, especially for women, in those days, was no part of their Religious life.

Mary MacKillop was instrumental in getting schools established but that was by no means all that she did, as the phrase 'social reformer' implies. Marie Foale points out that, although the Sisters always regarded education to be their main work, their Rule of life stated that:

> The Sisters must do all the good they can, and never see an evil without trying how they may remedy it.[5]

In addition to their work in schools, they were to engage in social work. Such a rule took them into areas of social concern that had nothing to do with education. Marie Foale points out that, 'once the Josephites entered the field of social welfare, they remained in it'.[6] The Sisters took charge of the newly opened Vincent de Paul orphanage. In 1867, Mary MacKillop assisted in opening a Refuge for destitute women and those in 'moral danger', and the same year, Father Woods and Mary started a Providence House for destitute adults and children. Lesley O'Brien writes:

> The Refuge took in former gaol inmates, former prosti-tutes and unmarried mothers ... Government welfare was practically non-existent in Australia before the 1900s ... To offer some relief Mary and Father Woods decided to open up another crisis accommodation centre ... It would cater for neglected children, young people ... homeless migrant women of all races and religions ... Mostly people at the Providence while looking for work or a permanent home.[7]

If government welfare was virtually non-existent before the 1900s, what other help would have been available? The Vincent de Paul Society helps many today who need money, clothes and food, but it was non-existent in Adelaide when Mary MacKillop was fighting against poverty. The first Vincent de Paul Conference in Adelaide was started in May 1884 at St Francis Xavier Cathedral. There was nothing like the network of help for people that there is nowadays.

The 'crisis accommodation centre' that Father Woods and Mary set up became known as a 'Providence'. The name 'Providence' would have been close to Mary's heart because of her mother's teaching to rely on Providence and her certainty that God would provide. But the Sisters did a lot of begging. They went about the streets of Adelaide on hot summer days. Geoffrey Hull describes them as having:

> ... carpet-bag in hand and perspiring under their heavy habits, risking public ridicule as they passed from door to door begging for themselves and for the poor.[8]

They didn't leave everything to Providence. But neither did they try to get Government assistance. Before 1900 the Sisters of St Joseph were the only non-governmental body offering residential care to the aged.

By managing an orphanage and setting up a Refuge and a Providence, Mary was showing the Government of the day where the need was, if they cared to see, and that there was an urgent need for Government money. Yet this does not mark her out as a social reformer who was anxious to change the law. She did not attempt to get money from the Government or to petition the Government, although Father Woods tried to get money for the orphanage. Mary MacKillop preferred to rely on Providence, believing that God would not let his children go hungry. Her only motive for doing this work with the poor was: 'Never see an evil without trying to remedy it.' This is a moral principle but hardly a principle to expect a Government department to operate on, since it addresses the individual. Josephites still act on this principle today. It marks them out as very caring, compassionate individuals who are courageous in speaking up for those on the margins of society.

When I say that Mary MacKillop was not a social reformer, I mean that she was not a reformer in the sense that Helen Prejean clearly is, campaigning and speaking out against the death penalty. It is certainly the case that Mary and the early Sisters had a reforming influence on the people they sought to help. Marie Foale remarks:

> One small sign of the success of the Refuge as a reforming agency was that … a small group of women decided to do something special to make reparation for their former misdemeanours … They formed a religious society known as the Magdalens of the Compassionate Heart of Mary.[9]

Although these reformed women regarded Julian Tenison Woods as their founder, they were conscious of the goodness of the Sisters and of Mary MacKillop, and they supported the Refuge by their needlework and shared all their possessions, much as the Sisters of St Joseph did. It is also the case that Helen Prejean, by her selfless giving of herself, especially to the families of those on Death Row, has had a reforming influence on people in situations that otherwise would have been degrading.

## Mary MacKillop's Mission to Prisoners

It was into this environment of caring for the poor and those who had no one to care for them that Mary also visited those in prison, and she got at least one of them released. It is Mary MacKillop's work in the Adelaide gaol that I find most interesting and moving. One of the first things she did after opening the Cathedral Hall School was to visit the Adelaide gaol. One sees her visiting truly lost souls and difficult cases. She was twenty-six – very young to be dealing with these criminals. Of her first visits to the gaol and the Government Destitute Asylum, Osmund Thorpe writes:

The officials did not quite know how to behave towards her, so great was their astonishment and embarrassment on meeting a nun. But soon their embarrassment and formality gave way to a warm admiration for her courage and generosity in devoting her young womanhood – she was twenty-six at the time – to works of charity usually so repugnant to human nature.[10]

Mary went to the prison fairly regularly on a Sunday. At least this was so in Adelaide. What did she feel, going into the prison? As far as I know, she has not written anywhere about her feelings. The prison must have been incredibly squalid. It was indeed a 'work of mercy'. She would surely have felt that she was among lost souls. She visited some very difficult prisoners, including two murderers. Sister Annette gives us this picture of a woman who had committed a murder:

There was a girl there whom they called 'Scotch Bella'. She came from Queensland … She dressed as a man for three years and worked on the roads. Nobody could do anything with her. She was sent to gaol in South Australia. Mother Mary got her out and she was brought to the Refuge. She was like a raving lunatic when they brought her there.[11]

Mary MacKillop got 'Scotch Bella' out of prison. She was definitely a very hard case for someone of twenty-six to try and reform. And Mary could have refused to take her to the Refuge. But she must have felt that, since no one could do anything with her, the Lord would prevail. There is no reference to her having got anyone else out of prison.

Paul Gardiner tells us that Bella calmed down and was eventually baptised, married and gave up drinking. What an amazing reforming influence Mary MacKillop and the Sisters must have had.

The other criminal, said to be one of the worst they had in Adelaide gaol, was also a condemned murderer. This is what Sister Annette writes:

There was in Adelaide a man named Fagan condemned to death for murder. Dr Reynolds – the bishop – and the priests went to see him but he was like a lion and had to be chained down. He was just like a wild animal. Mother Mary and Sister Felicitas went to see him. The warders told them not to go in. They went in and prayed and Mother was so affected that the tears poured down her face. This so moved him that he knelt down and prayed with them. At the beginning he was abrupt with Mother but he calmed down and became as gentle as a lamb. Mother prepared him for confession and Father Williams heard his confession and in the morning Mother went again with Sister Felicitas and he was without the chains and received Holy Communion between the two of them. Mother Mary wished to ascend the scaffold with him but this was not allowed. Father Williams however did ... I know many hardened sinners that others could not get but Mother Mary always prevailed on them.[12]

Mary MacKillop was no longer twenty-six when she visited Fagan. She was forty-one, but, even so, it must have taken a lot of courage to go into the cell when the warders had told them not to go in. It is hard to imagine this 'wild animal' being moved to pray with Mother Mary and becoming 'as gentle as a lamb'. Her presence must have been full of compassion and the love of Christ for this murderer. It was one of those rare and poignant moments in the inhuman prison conditions. Mary would never forget her effect on Fagan, nor his on her.

## The Bond Between Helen Prejean and Mary MacKillop

Helen Prejean was working with some of the most hardened criminals. The officials on Death Row did not know how to behave towards her to begin with, because she was a nun. She had a greater battle to be accepted than Mary MacKillop, probably because the people she was trying to help were thought of as being beyond help, so what she was doing was almost a waste of time. She found it impossible to get anyone out of prison. In fact she saw two go to the electric chair, who were later tragically shown to be innocent. Mary MacKillop had no such experience. It was her request 'to ascend the scaffold' with Fagan that is the remarkable connection with Sister Helen Prejean, who accompanied those on Death Row to the electric chair and whom we admire so much for doing so. She has accompanied six people on Death Row to their deaths. It is bringing the love of Jesus to those facing the death penalty that is the bond between Mary and Helen, and it took courage, which they both had. Helen writes about a very moving dialogue she had with Pat Sonnier, who was waiting to know if there was any chance of his being reprieved:

> 'No word yet', I tell him. 'Would you like to pray?'
>
> He nods his head. I don't remember the exact words of the prayer – a prayer I'm sure of essentials, forgiveness, courage, sustenance for the final big step should it come. When the prayer is over I say to him 'If you die, I want to be with you.'
>
> He says 'No, I don't want you to see it.'
>
> I say, 'I can't bear the thought that you would die without seeing one loving face. I will be the face of Christ for you. Just look at me.'[13]

It is obvious from what Helen says in the book that it took immense courage for her to be present at his execution. Mary MacKillop also wanted to be Christ to Fagan, and asked to go to the scaffold with him. She was not allowed to. A hundred and twenty-five years ago, a Religious going up onto the scaffold would probably have been shocking in the minds of some. Mary would have needed great courage to be with Fagan, as she wished. It was an amazing gift of grace just to make the request, which shows the lengths her love would take her. Geoffrey Hull comments:

> Mary MacKillop's reverence for every human creature meant that she was incapable of 'giving up' on anyone, even on a social outcast like Fagan who turned his back not only on his fellow man but on his Creator.[14]

Helen Prejean talks of Robert Lee Willie, one of the murderers she befriended on Death Row. He had also turned his back on his fellow man and on his Creator. In an interview she says:

> What intrigued me about him, I only had two months with him and truthfully when I heard what he had done I was just so appalled by the viciousness of it all ... He said when I walked in, 'Mmmmm, never thought I would be talking to no nun before ... I don't believe in that jail house religion, everybody sucking up to God and stuff'. I did give him a little cross which he put in his blue jeans pocket before he walked to his death.

He was very resistant to any approach by Helen. He seemed to feel no remorse for what he had done.

> He did say 'I hope my death gives you peace'. But he never said things like, 'God! The pain I've caused, please forgive me for what I've done ...'; but he did accept the little cross.[15]

It was hard work for her although the fact that he took the little cross must have given Helen a fleeting moment of hope. Jean Vanier's words also echo this hope:

> Everyone born of a man and a woman is a person, even if their deepest identity remains concealed beneath serious disturbance and depravity. The possibility always exists for any person to awaken to a life of relationship, however minimal, provided he or she is surrounded by respect and love.[16]

## The Courageous Compassion of Helen Prejean and Mary MacKillop

The impression that Mary made on the poor and needy was not that of a teacher, or an advisor, but of a friend. Mary had a genuine love for the poor. Those who came to her in any kind of distress were aware of her love for them and her longing to help them. Paul Gardiner writes:

> Her words of condolence ... were full of faith and hope and clearly came from the heart ... If anyone ever went to her in trouble and distress she would encourage and help them and draw the good that was in them out ... She had a deep feeling for all who were in distress of any kind.[17]

Above all she wanted to give the poor a sense of being accepted and of their self-worth, which meant that she always took people as she found them. There was nothing condescending about her manner. She wanted 'to draw the good that was in them out'.

After all, Mary had known from a very young age what it was like to have to depend on charity. Helen Prejean, like Mary MacKillop, stood supportively with those who were facing terrible pain. She says, 'I try to stand on common ground with people,' treating them as equals, who have fallen on hard times, the families of victims and the families of criminals, both facing the terrible things that people do to one another. Mary brought to Religious life a human quality that made her more than just an educator and certainly more than a social worker. A warmth of compassion and sincerity radiated from her.

Helen also managed to change Matthew Poncelet as Mary MacKillop seems to have changed Fagan from being a very violent man to someone who knew he needed forgiveness. Mary was very moved to see he was without chains when he received Holy Communion. Jean Vanier writes about Helen befriending Matthew:

> When Helen starts to demonstrate the faith she has in him and a relationship develops between them, Matthew is

transformed. Far more than impending execution and
death, her companionship in the depths of his darkness
shows him who he really is in his innermost being.[18]

Both Mary and Helen brought compassion into the prison scene.
Mary Cresp RSJ writes:

Sister Helen Prejean CSJ … work(ing) with prison inmates
to come to reconciliation and families of victims to healing
through forgiveness.[19]

Helen Prejean has a very challenging ministry to those on Death
Row, especially now, when she is trying to get the death penalty
abolished, that involves one of the hardest things to do: changing a
nation's consciousness and social attitudes. She writes:

I have no doubt that we will one day abolish the death
penalty in America. It will come sooner if people like me
who know the truth about executions do our work well
and educate the public. It will come slowly if we do not.
Because, finally I know that it is not a question of malice or
ill will or meanness of spirit that prompts our citizens to
support executions. It is, quite simply, that people don't
know the truth of what is going on.[20]

I believe that abolishing the death penalty is something Mary
MacKillop would have approved of. Mary MacKillop also met and
ministered to those who were condemned to death and as far as we
can tell she was able to prevail over the hardest characters. How did
she do it? She was really acting on Jesus' instruction (Matthew 25):

Come you who are blessed by my Father, inherit the
kingdom prepared for you from the foundation of the
world … I was in prison and you visited me. Then the
righteous will answer him, 'Lord … when was it that we
saw you … in prison and visited you.' And the king will
answer them, 'Truly, I tell you just as you did it to one of
the least of these, who are members of my family, you did
it to me'.

It must have taken outstanding courage and compassion to see Christ in the hardened faces of these condemned men who often had hostile attitudes to those who tried to help them. Yet there was no hint of judgment on the part of Helen Prejean or Mary MacKillop. There were moments, too, when the human spirit shone through even in the depraved lives of Pat Sonnier and Matthew Poncelet, and especially Fagan, who, in asking to be forgiven for what he had done, would have touched Mary's compassionate heart deeply.

Although Mary MacKillop has been represented in Adelaide as a social reformer, that was not what I found she had in common with Helen Prejean. It was their willingness to face and to work with those who, because of their heinous crimes, had cut them- selves off from family and friends and were waiting for the death penalty without hope. Both Mary MacKillop and Helen Prejean had great courage in taking the compassionate love of Christ into prisons and allowing themselves to become the face of Christ to these criminals. We do not know the extent of the reforming influence they had on the people they tried to help but it is the basis of the courageous bond between them.

# Further Reading

Thomas a Kempis, *The Imitation of Christ*, St Paul's, 1983

Frank Anderson MSC, *Jesus: Our Story*, Dove, 1994

Shirley du Boulay, *Teresa of Avila, An Extraordinary Life*, Bluebridge NY, 2004

Annice Callahan, *Karl Rahner's Spirituality of the Pierced Heart* (her doctoral thesis, that was published under the same name), Rowman & Littlefield, 1985

Annice Callahan, *Spiritual Guides for Today*, Crossroad Press NY, 1992

*Catechism of the Catholic Church*, St Paul's, 1994

Mary Cresp RSJ, *In the Spirit of Joseph*, pub. by the Sisters of St Joseph of the Sacred Heart, 2005

Jean-Pierre de Caussade, *The Sacrament of the Present Moment* trans. by Kitty Muggeridge, 1981

Marie Therese Foale RSJ, *The Josephite Story*, pub. by the Sisters of St Joseph, 1989

Paul Gardiner SJ, *An Extraordinary Australian Mary MacKillop*, E J Dwyer, 1994

Fayette Gosse, *Joanna and Robert, the Barr Smiths' Life in Letters 1853–1919*, Adelaide, 1996

St Ignatius Loyola SJ, *Letter on Obedience in Letters of St Ignatius Loyola*, St Loyola University Press, 1959

Daniel Lyne CP, *Mary MacKillop, Made in Australia*, Mary MacKillop Secretariat, 1994

Daniel Lyne CP, *Mary MacKillop Spirituality & Charisms*, pub. by St Joseph's Generalate 1993

Daniel Lyne CP, *Evangelical Poverty*, Edward and Shaw Pty. Ltd., 1983

Sheila McCreanor RSJ (ed.), *Mary MacKillop & Flora*, Sisters of St Joseph of the Sacred Heart, 2004

Margaret M. McKenna RSJ, *With Grateful Hearts*, pub. by the Sisters of St Joseph of the Sacred Heart, 2009

Mary MacKillop, *Mother Mary's Circulars to the Sisters*, Sisters of St Joseph, 1976

Mary MacKillop, *Meditations*, St Vincent's Boys' Home, 1947

Mary MacKillop, *A Book of Instructions*, Sydney, 1907

William Modystack, *Mary MacKillop, A Unique Australian*, Rigby, 1986

Henri Nouwen, *The Way of the Heart*, Darton, Longman and Todd, 2001

Lesley O'Brien, *Mary MacKillop Unveiled*, Collins Dove, 1994

Diarmuid O'Murchu, *Poverty, Celibacy and Obedience,* The Crossroad Publishing Company, 1999

Pope Paul VI, *on Joseph* (Encyclical)

Pope Pius XI, *Caritate Christi Compulsi* (Encyclical On the Sacred Heart 3 May 1932)

Pope Pius XII, *The Eucharistic Heart of Jesus* (Encyclical)

Pope Pius XII, *The Sacred Heart* (Encyclical Letter *Haurietis Aquas* 1956)

Karl Rahner, *Theological Investigations* Vol. III & Vol. VIII, Darton, Longman and Todd, 1967

Karl Rahner, *Christianity in the Market Place,* Sheed & Ward, 1966

Sandra Schneiders IHM, *Selling All* Vol. II Religious Life in a New Millennium, Paulist Press, 2001

Michael J Walsh, *The Heart of Christ in the Writings of Karl Rahner,* Rome, 1977

Simone Weil, *Waiting on God,* Fontana Books, 1959

Pauline Wicks RSJ, *God Will Take Care of Us All,* St Paul's, 2009

Pauline Wicks RSJ (ed.), *Mary MacKillop Inspiration For Today,* Trustees of the Sisters of St Joseph of the Sacred Heart, 2005

# Notes

## Chapter 1

1 *Daily Telegraph*, Sydney, 11 August 1909
2 Cardinal Moran was Archbishop of Sydney from 1884 until his death in 1911
3 *Life and Letters of Mother Mary of the Cross*, by a Sister of St Joseph, Westmead, 1916, p.398
4 Mary MacKillop, *Circular to the Sisters*, 19 March 1893, Mount Street, 1976, p.179
5 Victor Feehan and Ann MacDonnell, *In Search of Alexander MacKillop*, St Joseph Publications, 1994, for further biographical information
6 Sheila McCreanor RSJ (ed.), *Mary MacKillop and Flora* (Correspondence between Mary MacKillop and her mother, Flora McDonald MacKillop), 27 Nov. 1866, Sisters of St Joseph of the Sacred Heart, 2004, p.11
7 Mary MacKillop, Letter to Monsignor Kirby at Rome, 1873
8 The Sisters at Le Puy were founded about 1650. For further information see Mary Cresp RSJ, *In the Spirit of Joseph*, Sisters of St Joseph of the Sacred Heart, 2005
9 Bishop Lawrence Bonaventure Sheil was Bishop of Adelaide from 1866 to 1871. He came from Ireland
10 Sheila McCreanor RSJ, *ibid*. Mary MacKillop, letter to her mother, 26 February 1872
11 Mary MacKillop to Franchi, 20 May 1875, MacKillop, *Letterbook*
12 Bishop Matthew Quinn, Bishop of Bathurst 1865–1885
13 Mary MacKillop, letter to Father Woods, September 1871
14 Mary MacKillop, Circular to the Sisters, 11 December 1880
15 Archbishop Roger Vaughan of Sydney 1877–1883
16 Dean Kenny was a friend of her father's. He gave up his house on the property for the Sisters and went to live in a little cottage
17 Quoted by Sister M. Peter in her book *Dauntless Daughter of Desires*, Sisters of St Joseph of the Sacred Heart, 1965, p.24
18 Bishop (Archbishop) of Adelaide Christopher Augustine Reynolds died in 1893
19 Abnormally painful menstruation

## Chapter 2

1 Evelyn Pickering RSJ, *Mary and Julian, Their Letters 1862–1868,* The Generalate, Sisters of St Joseph of the Sacred Heart, 1989

2 *Mother Mary's Circulars to the Sisters,* Mother House, North Sydney, 1976

3 Mary MacKillop, *Meditations for the Use of the Sisters of St Joseph of the Sacred Heart,* printed at St Vincent's Boys Home, Westmead, Sydney, 1947

4 William Modystack, *Mary MacKillop, A Woman Before Her Time,* Rigby, 1982

5 Evelyn Underhill, *Concerning the Inner Life with The House of the Soul,* Methuen, 1947, p.3

6 Gerard Henderson, *Sydney Morning Herald,* 10 January 1995

7 Mary MacKillop, *Mother Mary's Circulars to the Sisters,* 19 March 1893

8 There was a 'coming of age' throughout Christendom in the 1960s. The aftermath of Vatican II could be described by this phrase

9 David Walker, 'The French Influence', *The Australasian Catholic Record,* Vol LV No.1, 1978, pp.28–35

10 Anonymous, 'Memory Portraits of Mother Mary', *The Garland,* June 1938

11 Mary MacKillop, *Meditations for the Use of the Sisters of St Joseph of the Sacred Heart,* 'For the Last Day of St Joseph's Month', p.83. She speaks of St Joseph as submitting to the will of God as a model to be followed

12 Anne Marie Power RSJ, 'We are her people', 1982, p.32

13 Daniel Lyne CP, *Mary MacKillop, Made in Australia,* Mary MacKillop Secretariat, 1994, pp.34

14 Thomas Merton, *The Asian Journal,* Sheldon Press, 1974, Appendix ix

15 Jean-Pierre de Caussade, *The Sacrament of the Present Moment,* trans. by Kitty Muggeridge from the original text of the treatise on *Self Abandonment to Divine Providence,* Collins Fount, 1981, p.39

16 Simone Weil, *Waiting on God,* Fontana, 1959, p.90

17 'Congregation for the Causes of the Saints', Mary of the Cross MacKillop, *Positio,* Vols. I–III, Rome, 1989

18 Mary MacKillop, *Meditations for the Use of the Sisters of St Joseph of the Sacred Heart,* 'Monday Morning – The Agony', pp.7–11

19 Mary MacKillop, *Meditations for the Use of the Sisters of St Joseph of the Sacred Heart,* pp.41–44

20 Daniel Lyne, *Mary MacKillop, Spirituality and Charisms,* St Joseph's Generalate, Sydney, 1993, p.100

21 Bargil Pixner, *With Jesus through Galilee According to the Fifth Gospel,* Corazin Publishing, 1992

22  The non-ownership of property was modified by the Vatican in 1874

23  Mary MacKillop, *Meditations for the Use of the Sisters of St Joseph of the Sacred Heart*, p.76

24  Carmel Leavy OP and Rosalie O'Neill RSJ, *Gathered in God's Name: New Horizons in Australian Religious Life*, Crossing Press, 1996

25  Janet McCalman, *Mary MacKillop: A Reflection on Her Life, a Symposium*, 'Australia in the time of Mother Mary MacKillop', The Victorian Branch of the Mary MacKillop Foundation, 1995, p.6

26  Simone Weil, 'Human Personality', *Selected Essays, 1934–45*, chosen and trans. by Richard Rees, OUP, 1962, p.27

27  Simone Weil, *Waiting on God*, p.63

28  Daniel Lyne CP, *Mary MacKillop: Made in Australia*, p.22

29  Mary MacKillop, Letter to Fr Poupinel, 9 May 1873 (quoted by Daniel Lyne in *Mary MacKillop: Made in Australia*, p.39)

## Chapter 3

1  Isaiah 55:9

2  I have already spoken about the difficulty today with the Will of God theology in *Mary MacKillop and the Will of God*

3  Mary MacKillop, *Circular to the Sisters*, 21 May 1907

4  Evelyn Underhill was under the influence of the Roman Catholic theologian, Baron Friedrich von Hugel

5  Thomas a Kempis, *The Imitation of Christ*

6  An Act of Consecration to the Sacred Heart is part of the Devotion that invites God to take every one of our faculties including our wills

7  Daniel Lyne CP, *Mary MacKillop, Spirituality and Charisms*, St Joseph's Generalate, 1983, p.167

8  Evelyn Underhill, *Concerning the Inner Life*, Methuen, 1926, p.7

9  Mary MacKillop, a letter to her mother 14 September 1869, in Sheila McCreanor (ed.), *Mary MacKillop & Flora*, Sisters of St Joseph of the Sacred Heart, 2004, p.29

10  Evelyn Underhill, *The Light of Christ*, Longmans, Green & Co, 1944, p.82

11  Mary MacKillop, a letter to Monsignor Kirby, Ascension Thursday 1873

12  Evelyn Underhill, *Concerning the Inner Life*, p.27

13  *ibid*, p.26

14  *ibid*, p.41

## Chapter 4

1 Joan Chittister OSB, *Twelve Steps To Inner Freedom, Humility Revisited*, Benetvision, USA, 2003, used with permission

2 Esther de Waal, *Lost in Wonder*, John Garratt Publishing, Victoria, 2003

3 Mary MacKillop to Julian Tenison Woods, 3 June 1870

4 Mary MacKillop to the Sisters, 19 March 1893

5 Mary MacKillop, *A Book of Instructions for the Use of the Sisters of St Joseph of the Sacred Heart*, Boys' Industrial Home Print, Sydney, 1907, pp.25–29

6 Paul Gardiner, *Cause of Canonisation of the Servant of God, Mary of the Cross MacKillop (1842–1909), Foundress of the Sisters of St Joseph of the Sacred Heart*, Positio super Virtutibus, Rome, 1989, Congregation for the Causes of the Saints, p.312

7 Mary MacKillop to Woods, 3 June 1870

8 *ibid*. The original Rule written by Julian Tenison Woods stated that Sisters were to 'consider themselves the least among all religious orders'. The precise meaning is not known, but it may have been purely pragmatic – Australia was a young country, and the Sisters of St Joseph were a young Institute

9 Paul Gardiner, *An Extraordinary Australian: Mary MacKillop, The Authorised Biography*, E. J. Dwyer, 1993, p.402

10 Mary MacKillop, *A Book of Instructions for the Use of the Sisters of St Joseph of the Sacred Heart*, p.7

11 Paul Tillich, *Courage to Be*, Collins, 1962, pp.153–154

12 Joan Chittister OSB, *Twelve Steps To Inner Freedom, Humility Revisited*, p.23

13 Esther de Waal, *Lost in Wonder*, p.82

14 Karl Rahner, *Ignatius Loyola*, Collins, 1979, pp.23–24

15 Paul Gardiner, *An Extraordinary Australian: Mary MacKillop, The Authorised Biography*, p.178 Gardiner refers to Mary MacKillop having studied Ignatius Loyola's *Letter on Obedience*

16 Pope John Paul II, *Guardian of the Redeemer: Apostolic Exhortation on the Person and Mission of St Joseph in the Life of Christ and of the Church*, St Paul's Books and Media, Boston, 1989. 'St Joseph is proof … it is enough to have the common, simple human virtues but they need to be true and authentic.' Quoted from Paul VI's discourse, 19 March 1969, No.29

17 Mary MacKillop to the Sisters, 19 March 1873

18 Paul Gardiner, *The Positio*, p.312

19 Mary MacKillop to the Sisters, 19 March 1893

20 Mary MacKillop, *A Book of Instructions for the Use of the Sisters of St Joseph of the Sacred Heart*, p.5

21 *Resource Material from the Archives of the Sisters of St Joseph of the Sacred Heart*, Issue No 10 p.30

22 Rosemary Haughton, *The Passionate God*, Darton, Longman and Todd, 1982, p.328

23 Jean Vanier, *The Scandal of Service*, Darton, Longman and Todd, 1997, p.51

24 Mary MacKillop to the Sisters, 25 September 1873

25 Mary MacKillop to the Sisters, 4 September 1906

26 Gardiner, *The Positio*, p.32

27 Chittister, *Twelve Steps to Inner Freedom*, p.33

28 Huston Smith, *The World's Religion*, Harper Collins, 1991, p.387

29 Chittister, *Twelve Steps to Inner Freedom*, p.58

30 Chittister, *Twelve Steps to Inner Freedom*, p.20

31 Mary MacKillop, *A Book of Instructions for the Use of the Sisters of St Joseph of the Sacred Heart*, p.59

## Chapter 5

1 Marie Therese Foale RSJ, *The Josephite Story*, The Sisters of St Joseph, 1989, p.18

2 Julian Tenison Woods was given no opportunity to defend his Rules, which had been drafted with Australian conditions in mind. The Sisters were to be mobile and available to be sent anywhere there was a need. Ownership of property would be a hindrance to the objective for which they had been founded.

3 Marie Foale refers to a link between the Josephites' and the Franciscans' understanding of poverty in *The Josephite Story*, p.130

4 *Resource Material from the Archives of the Sisters of St Joseph of the Sacred Heart*, Issue No.8, p.63

5 *Resource Material from the Archives of the Sisters of St Joseph of the Sacred Heart*, Issue No.3 (Revised), p.4

6 From a letter to Cardinal Franchi from Mary MacKillop 30 August.1874), in *Resource Material from the Archives of the Sisters of St Joseph of the Sacred Heart*, Issue No.8, p.5

7 *Resource Material from the Archives of the Sisters of St Joseph of the Sacred Heart*, Issue No.3 (Revised), p.38

8 *Resource Material from the Archives of the Sisters of St Joseph of the Sacred Heart*, Issue No.3 (Revised), p.64

9 *Catechism of the Catholic Church*, St Paul's, 1994, p.341

10 From a letter from Tenison Woods to Mary MacKillop 13 June 1875, *Resource Material from the Archives of the Sisters of St Joseph of the Sacred Heart,* Issue No.8 p.67

11 From a letter from Tenison Woods to Mary MacKillop 24 June 1875, *Resource Material from the Archives of the Sisters of St Joseph of the Sacred Heart,* Issue No.8. p.68

12 Julian Tenison Woods, *The Spirit of the Institute,* 1870, in *Resource Material from the Archives of the Sisters of St Joseph of the Sacred Heart,* Issue No.3 (Revised), p.64

13 Mary MacKillop, *Adaptation of the Rules of 1867,* in *Resource Material from the Archives of the Sisters of St Joseph of the Sacred Heart,* Issue No.8, p.16

14 *ibid.* p.17

15 I am grateful to Sr Marie Foale for information regarding finances, when she spoke to Sisters at the New South Wales Province Centre on 12 October 2008

16 Diarmuid O'Murchu, *Poverty, Chastity and Obedience,* Crossroads Publishing Co, 1999, p.80

17 Mary MacKillop, *Mother Mary's Circulars to the Sisters,* 19 March 1893, Sisters of St Joseph, 1976, p.177

18 *ibid.* p.166

19 Matthew 8:20

20 Sandra Schneiders IHM, *Selling All, Religious Life in a New Millennium,* Vol.II, Paulist Press, 2001, p.258

21 Mary MacKillop, *Mother Mary's Circulars to the Sisters,* 19 March 1893, p.68

22 Mary MacKillop, *Mother Mary's Circulars to the Sisters,* 19 March 1893, p.69

23 Audrey Gibson and Kieran Kneaves, *Praying with Louise de Marillac,* p.84

24 Many Sisters have similar experiences of poverty. This is not an isolated instance

## Chapter 6

1 Pope Pius XII, *Encyclical on the Sacred Heart,* quoted by Rev. Robert Nash SJ in *The Sacred Heart,* Australian Catholic Truth Society, 1963, p.8

2 *ibid. Haurietis Aquas,* also quoted by Robert Nash

3 Karl Rahner, *Ignatian Spirituality and Devotion to the Heart of Jesus,* p.132

4 Mary MacKillop, *Mother Mary's Circulars to the Sisters.* North Sydney, 1976

5  Karl Rahner, *Behold This Heart: Preliminaries to a Theology of Devotion to the Sacred Heart,* in his *Theological Investigations,* Vol. II, trans. by Karl H and Boniface Kruger, Darton, Longman and Todd, 1967, pp.321–330

6  *ibid.* p.330

7  Proverbs 4:23

8  Mary MacKillop, *Circular,* 21 May 1907, p.245

9  *ibid.* Feast of the Annunciation, p.5

10  Daniel Lyne CP, *Mary MacKillop,* North Sydney, 1983, p.178

11  *ibid.* p.170

12  Mary MacKillop, *Circular,* 21 May 1878, p.88

13  *ibid. Circular,* Feast of the Annunciation 1873, p.5

14  *ibid. Circular,* May 1877, p.89

15  *ibid. Circular,* 17 December 1883, p.123

16  Mary MacKillop, *ibid.* 6 August 1870, p.2

17  Mary MacKillop, *ibid.* 1 April 1890, p.149

18  Paul Gardiner, *The Positio,* Vol. III, p.25

19  Mary MacKillop, *Book of Instructions,* 1907, quoted by Daniel Lyne p.177

20  *ibid.* quoted by Daniel Lyne, p.178

21  *ibid.* quoted by Daniel Lyne, p.178

22  *ibid.* quoted by Daniel Lyne, p.178

23  A Sister of St Joseph, *Life and Letters of Mother Mary of the Cross* (*MacKillop*), Westmead, 1916, p.25

24  *ibid.* Letter from Mary MacKillop to Julian Tenison Woods, 1870

25  Mary MacKillop, *Circular,* 5 June 1874, p.71

26  *ibid. Circular,* 26 September 1873, p.45

27  Henri Nouwen, *The Way of the Heart,* Darton, Longman and Todd, 2001, pp.65–66

28  Mary MacKillop, *Circular,* 21 May 1907, p.247

29  Mary MacKillop, *ibid.*

30  Song of Songs 6:3

31  Mary MacKillop, *ibid.*

32  Karl Rahner, *Unity – Love – Mystery,* p.233

33  Karl Rahner, *ibid.*

## Chapter 7

1  Sandra Schneiders IHM, *Selling All, Vol. II, Religious Life in a New Millennium,* Paulist Press, 2001

2  Mary MacKillop, *A Little Book of Instructions,* Westmead, 1907, p.68

3  St Ignatius Loyola, 'Letter on Obedience' from *Letters of St Ignatius Loyola,* selected and trans. by William J Young SJ, Loyola University Press, 1959, pp.287–295. The letter is also obtainable from the Internet

4  Paul Gardiner, *An Extraordinary Australian: Mary MacKillop, The Author-ised Biography,* 1993, p.178

5  Mary MacKillop, *Circular,* 16 October 1885, *Mother Mary's Circulars to the Sisters,* Sisters of St Joseph, 1976

6  The 'Letter on Obedience' was written as a result of an unfortunate situation in the Province of Portugal, where the provincial Rodrigues had a following that was attached to him in a way that could not be described as spiritual

7  Mary MacKillop, *Circular* to Sisters in NSW, 16 December 1900

8  Mary MacKillop, *Circular* to Sisters in SA, 17 December 1883

9  Mary MacKillop, *Circular* to the Sisters, 6 August 1870

10  Mary MacKillop, *Circular* to the Sisters, Feast of the Annunciation 1873

11  Mary MacKillop, *Rules of the Institute of the Sisters of St Joseph,* 1867, J J Cronin, p.32

12  Mary MacKillop, *Circular* to the Sisters, 17 December 1883

13  Rev. Dr I F Campbell was Rector of Scots College in Rome. Mary could write freely to him regarding her troubles. See *Mary MacKillop in Challenging Times 1883–1899,* a collection of letters arranged and ed. Sheila McCreanor RSJ, Sisters of St Joseph of the Sacred Heart, 2006

14  Bishop Reynolds was Bishop of Adelaide 1873–1893. His relations with Mary changed from being cordial to being unfriendly and critical

15  Mary MacKillop, Circular to the Sisters, 17 December 1906

## Chapter 8

1  Shirley du Boulay, *Teresa of Avila, An Extraordinary Life,* Bluebridge, 2004

2  Fayette Gosse, *Joanna and Robert, The Barr Smiths' Life in Letters 1853–1919,* ed. Fayette Gosse, Barr Smith Press, 1996

3  Sheila McCreanor (ed.), *Mary MacKillop & Flora,* Sisters of St Joseph of the Sacred Heart, 2004, p.87

4  William Modystack, *Mary MacKillop, A Unique Australian,* Rigby, 1986, p.103

5  Fayette Gosse, *ibid.* p.xxvii

6  Letter from the Archives, North Sydney

7  Fayette Gosse, *ibid.* p.28

8  *ibid.* William Modystack, *Mary MacKillop, A Unique Australian,* p.103

9  Letter from Mary MacKillop to Annie MacKillop, 18 September 1873 in *Letterbook*

10  Letter from the Archives, North Sydney

11  *ibid.* William Modystack, *Mary MacKillop, A Unique Australian,* p.102

12  Fayette Gosse, *ibid*. p.188
13  *ibid*. William Modystack, *Mary MacKillop, A Unique Australian,* p.258
14  *ibid*. William Modystack, *Mary MacKillop, A Unique Australian,* p.263
15  *ibid*. William Modystack, *Mary MacKillop, A Unique Australian,* p.263

## Chapter 9

1  Positio, *Mary of the Cross MacKillop,* Vol. III, Rome, 1989, p.2
2  Andrew Louth, *The Wisdom of the Greek Fathers,* Lion, 1997, p.6
3  Mary MacKillop, *Mother Mary's Circulars to the Sisters,* Sisters of St Joseph, 21 May 1877, p.88
4  Quoted by Shirley du Boulay, *Teresa of Avila,* Bluebridge, 1991, p.227
5  Oliver Davies, *The Wisdom of Meister Eckhart,* Lion, 1999, p.40
6  Thomas a Kempis, *The Imitation of Christ,* St Pauls, 1995, Book IV, ch.13, p.384
7  *Circular to the Sisters,* 19 March 1893, p.175
8  Positio, quoted by Paul Gardiner, p.66
9  Mary MacKillop, Feast of the Purification, *Meditations For Every Day in the Week and Other Occasions,* St Vincent's Boys' Home, 1947, p.95
10  *ibid*. Oliver Davies, p.10
11  Mary MacKillop, *Meditations, ibid.* For the Last Day of St Joseph's Month, p.76
12  Mary MacKillop, *Circulars, ibid.* Feast of the Annunciation 1873, p.4
13  *ibid*. Oliver Davies, p.20
14  *ibid*. Positio, p.6
15  *ibid*. Positio, p.72
16  Nan Merrill, *Psalms for Praying,* Continuum, 2004, p.100
17  *ibid*. Positio p.80
18  Mary MacKillop
19  Robert J Wicks *Crossing the Desert,* Sorin Books, 2007, p.90
20  Mary MacKillop, *Letterbook,* Letter to Father Woods, 14 October 1871, Sisters of St Joseph Archives
21  *ibid*. Mary MacKillop, *Circulars,* Circular to the Sisters, 14 December 1890, p.162
22  *ibid*. Mary MacKillop, *Circulars,* Circular, 1 April 1890, pp.148–149
23  E J Cuskelly MSC, *Walking the Way of Jesus,* St Paul's, 1999, p.80
24  *ibid*. Positio, p.116
25  *ibid*. Robert J Wicks, p.7

## Chapter 10

1  Helen Prejean CSJ, *Dead Man Walking,* Fount, 1993

2 Helen Prejean CSJ, *Death of the Innocents*, Random House, 2005, Preface

3 Albert Camus, quoted by Helen Prejean, *Dead Man Walking*, p.45

4 *Life and Letters of Mother Mary of the Cross (MacKillop)*, a Sister of St Joseph of the Sacred Heart, Westmead, 1916, p.84

5 Marie Therese Foale RSJ, *Think of the Ravens*, Sisters of St Joseph of the Sacred Heart (SA), 2001 p.2

6 *ibid.*Marie Therese Foale RSJ, p.5

7 Lesley O'Brien, *Mary MacKillop Unveiled*, Collins Dove, 1994, p.53

8 Geoffrey Hull, *Building the Kingdom: Mary MacKillop and Social Justice*, Dove, 1994, p.10

9 *ibid.* Marie Therese Foale RSJ, p.15

10 Osmond Thorpe, *Mary MacKillop; Mother Mary of the Cross*, Burns & Oates, 1967 pp.78–79

11 *ibid.* Paul Gardiner SJ, p.241

12 *ibid.* Paul Gardiner SJ, pp.241–242

13 Helen Prejean CSJ, *Dead Man Walking*, p.47

14 *ibid.* Geoffrey Hull, p.25

15 The title of an interview with Helen Prejean is a frontline interview, 'Angel on Death Row', from the Internet

16 Jean Vanier, *Made for Happiness*, trans. by Kathryn Spink, Darton Longman and Todd, 2001, p.182

17 *ibid.* Paul Gardiner SJ, p.241

18 *ibid.* Jean Vanier, p.182

19 Mary Cresp RSJ, *In the Spirit of Joseph*, Sisters of St Joseph of the Sacred Heart, North Sydney, 2005, p.150

20 Helen Prejean CSJ, *Dead Man Walking*, p.252–253

# JOSEPHITES TODAY

Sisters of St Joseph of the Sacred Heart live by the motto of their founders, St Mary of the Cross MacKillop and Fr Julian Tenison Woods: Never see a need without trying to do something about it. Today they work with Associates and co-workers to meet many different needs.

Their influence is world-wide. There are Josephites in East Timor, Peru, Brazil, Scotland and Ireland, as well as New Zealand and Australia, where they were founded. They are an Australian order. Their work in these countries is varied. One of the poorest places where they work is East Timor. A group of Sisters and Associates and others help with education. Their schools have virtually nothing. Josephites have provided them with books in their Tetun language and they have trained East Timorese teachers.

In Peru, Sisters and Associates work with the local women to produce hand-crafted articles for sale in Australia through Ethica Accessories. In this way they are helping poor women to become more financially independent.

Josephites have set up parish-based programs in Brazil to support and train leaders in a disadvantaged area.

In Australia and New Zealand, Sisters and Associates work together in schools as teachers, administrators and chaplains. They also provide liaison between parents and the school. They work with Aboriginal Australians to give them better health and education. They assist women who have been victims of human 'trafficking'. They engage with refugees from the Sudan. They look after adults with special needs, enabling them to go out to work and to live as independently as possible.

Young people in Sydney have formed a group, Josephite Community Aid (JCA). They go where they are needed. They work along with refugees to help them set up a house so they can begin to feel at home in a strange country.

Josephites are also active in caring for the elderly and working in rural communities, where women especially are in need of companionship.

There has been a Josephite presence in Ireland for longer than in Scotland. In both places they keep the flame of St Mary MacKillop's heart alive among the people.

## FOR MORE INFORMATION

Contact the Josephite website on <u>www.sosj.org.au</u>

or write to: St Joseph's Congregational Administration Centre,
PO Box 1508,
North Sydney,
New South Wales, Australia 2059

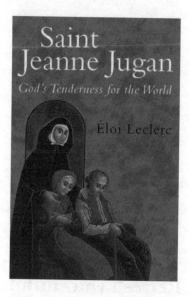

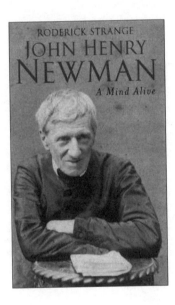